Exploring Gun Use
in America

Titles in the series

Exploring Gun Use in America

VOLUME 2

The Firearms Industry

GREENWOOD PRESS
Westport, Connecticut · London

Library of Congress Cataloging-in-Publication Data

Exploring gun use in America / Creative Media Applications.
      p. cm. — (Middle school reference)
    Includes bibliographical references and index.
    Contents: v. 1. The second amendment — v. 2. The firearms industry —
    v. 3. Children and guns — v. 4. Public opinion.
    ISBN 0–313–32896–X (alk. paper: set) — ISBN 0–313–32897–8 (alk. paper: vol. 1) —
    ISBN 0–313–32898–6 (alk. paper: vol. 2) — ISBN 0–313–32899–4 (alk. paper: vol. 3) —
    ISBN 0–313–32900–1 (alk. paper: vol. 4)
        1. Gun control — United States. 2. Firearms — Law and legislation — United States.
        3. Gun control — United States — Public opinion. 4. Public opinion — United States.
        I. Creative Media Applications. II. Series.
    HV7436.E94   2004
    363.33′0973 — dc22   2003067750

British Library Cataloguing in Publication Data is available.

Copyright © 2004 by Greenwood Publishing Group, Inc.

All rights reserved. No portion of this book may be
reproduced, by any process or technique, without the
express written consent of the publisher.

Library of Congress Catalog Card Number: 2003067750
ISBN: 0–313–32896–X (set)
      0–313–32897–8 (vol. 1)
      0–313–32898–6 (vol. 2)
      0–313–32899–4 (vol. 3)
      0–313–32900–1 (vol. 4)

First published in 2004

Greenwood Press, 88 Post Road West, Westport, CT 06881
An imprint of Greenwood Publishing Group, Inc.
www.greenwood.com

Printed in the United States of America

The paper used in this book complies with the
Permanent Paper Standard issued by the National
Information Standards Organization (Z39.48–1984).

10 9 8 7 6 5 4 3 2 1

A Creative Media Applications, Inc. Production
WRITER: Mathew Kachur
DESIGN AND PRODUCTION: Alan Barnett, Inc.
EDITOR: Matt Levine
COPYEDITOR: Laurie Lieb
PROOFREADER: Betty Pessagno
INDEXER: Nara Wood
ASSOCIATED PRESS PHOTO RESEARCHER: Yvette Reyes
CONSULTANT: Eugene Volokh, Professor of Law, UCLA School of Law

PHOTO CREDITS:
AP/Wide World Photographs *pages:* vii, viii, 1, 2, 6, 8, 11, 70, 76, 81, 82, 86, 89, 94, 97, 99, 100, 103, 105,
    107, 108, 111, 113, 114, 116, 118, 120, 123
© Hulton Archives/Getty Images *pages:* 5, 15, 21, 22, 28, 31, 59, 61, 63, 64, 66
© North Wind Picture Archives *pages:* 18, 35, 40, 43, 49, 56
© CORBIS *page:* 25
© PictureHistory *pages:* 37, 47, 50
© Bettmann/CORBIS *pages:* 53, 69, 73, 75, 79
© AFP/CORBIS *page:* 91

Table of Contents

INTRODUCTION

The manufacture of firearms is a major industry in the United States. In the year 2000, American firearms firms manufactured an estimated 1.2 million handguns, 1.5 million rifles, and almost 1 million shotguns. For the last thirty-five years, American companies have produced between 2.5 and 5.7 million guns every year. Guns are everywhere in the United States; a 1997 study reported that more than one-third of all American households owned guns, with the total number of weapons approaching 200 million.

A government official of Miami-Dade County, Florida, holds up a handgun involved in the accidental, fatal shooting of a child in January 1999. The official was announcing a lawsuit against firearms manufacturers, brought in an effort to get them to make safer, childproof guns.

This display of bullets illustrated Massachusetts lawmakers' 2000 proposal to require gun manufacturers to supply a previously shot bullet and shell casing for every gun sold. This would help law enforcement officials match bullets collected from future crime scenes with the registered guns from which they were shot.

The American firearms industry has a long and proud history. Gun manufacturers can boast of an impressive record of technological innovation, including the invention or improvement of cartridges, repeating rifles, breechloaders, machine guns, and other automatic weapons. In the 1800s, the firearms industry was one of the first manufacturing sectors in the United States to use precision measuring tools, machine production, and division of labor; the result was a trend-setting example of mass-production techniques. Private companies such as Colt, Remington, Winchester, Spencer, Sharps, and Smith & Wesson became famous throughout the world as symbols of the cleverness of American inventors. At the same time, gun manufacturers pioneered cooperation between private companies and the government in research and development at the nationally owned armory in Springfield, Massachusetts. Public and private gun producers helped the United States arm its soldiers and emerge triumphant from most of the wars that the nation fought.

Despite this proud history, the production of firearms creates a great deal of controversy. This is because the main purpose of guns—outside sport shooting and collecting—is to provide an efficient way to destroy people or animals, or threaten to destroy them. Automobiles also cause many injuries and deaths in the United States, but this is not their primary purpose. The unique destructive capability of guns causes many Americans to dislike firearms intensely. Supporters of gun control cite the gun as the weapon of choice in political assassinations, street crime, attacks in schools, and suicides. On the other hand, their opponents point out that the overwhelming majority of firearms are used responsibly for target shooting, hunting, national defense, and individual protection. Many people hold both these views at the same time.

Manufacturers of guns in the United States have a difficult task. They clearly provide a desired product that fills a need in American society. Like producers of any other item, the gun industry wants to sell as many units and make as great a profit as possible. At the same time, good citizenship and the fear of government restrictions force manufacturers to consider the negative role of guns in American society. In recent years, trigger locks, ballistic fingerprinting, and "smart guns" have all been proposed to make guns "safer." Firearms manufacturers have to respond to these demands in a way that balances safety and profit.

Gun manufacturing has always been an erratic profession, but never more so than in the twenty-first century. Although guns remain popular, critics of the firearms industry have begun taking gun manufacturers to court for failing to include safety devices that could prevent injuries caused by the use or misuse of their products. Some of these lawsuits have succeeded, and judges and juries have begun to hold gun manufacturers and dealers liable for their actions. Large cash awards have threatened some major firearms companies with bankruptcy. In response, in 2003, the gun industry sponsored legislation in Congress, known as HR 1056/S, which would grant legal immunity not only to gun manufacturers but also to gun dealers, distributors, and trade associations. The heated controversy over this law indicates that the firearms industry will remain at the center of arguments over the role of guns in America for the foreseeable future.

Note: All metric conversions in this book are approximate.

CHAPTER 1

Firearms in the United States

irearms are weapons that use a powder charge to shoot something, usually a bullet or shell, from a straight tube. The force that propels the bullet or shell is usually created when gunpowder is ignited. Firearms can be divided into two types: *small arms* and *heavy arms* (known as *artillery*). Small arms can be further separated into long guns and handguns. *Long guns,* such as rifles, shotguns, and muskets, are usually fired from the shoulder. *Handguns,* such as pistols and revolvers, are designed to fit easily in one hand and can be fired that way. They usually measure less than 18 inches (45 centimeters) in length.

Firearms are activated by pulling a *trigger. Single-shot* guns are just that; they have to be slowly and carefully reloaded in order to fire a second shot. On the other hand, *repeating firearms* allow the shooter or some mechanism on the gun to reload quickly after a shot has been fired. Manually repeating firearms require the shooter to operate a bolt, lever, slide, or pump that reloads a fresh shell or cartridge (which holds the bullet and the powder to propel it) from the magazine into the chamber and cocks the gun.

This 9mm semiautomatic handgun is displayed along with its magazine. The 9mm designation refers to the diameter (9 millimeters) of the inside of the gun's barrel. Semiautomatic means that when the gun is fired, it automatically loads another bullet, ready for firing, from its magazine, which is loaded into the gun beforehand.

Semiautomatic guns do this automatically when they fire. Each time the trigger is pulled, they fire, eject the empty case, and reload a new cartridge. Semiautomatic guns fire only one bullet for each squeeze of the trigger. This is different from *fully automatic* guns, sometimes known as *machine guns*. Machine guns fire more than one bullet for each trigger pull—usually between 400 and 1,600 rounds of ammunition per minute. Some guns can be set to be either semiautomatic or fully automatic; these are known as *select fire weapons*.

Caliber and Cartridge

People discuss the size of a gun based on its *caliber,* which is the measurement of the inside of a gun barrel (or *bore*). For example, a .45-caliber revolver has a barrel with an inside diameter of 0.45 inches (11 millimeters). American rifle calibers usually range from .17 to .46. Some confusion exists because American measurements, which use inches and hundredths of an inch, differ from those of the rest of the world, which use millimeters and centimeters. In addition, caliber is sometimes determined by the diameter of the grooves in the rifle barrel, which is slightly larger than the figure for the barrel.

A cartridge is not the same as a bullet, although the two words are now often used interchangeably. A *bullet* is simply the projectile shot from a gun. In order to fire bullets, a gun requires gunpowder to propel the bullets and primer to ignite the gunpowder. Before 1800, these were entirely separate ingredients. A *cartridge,* also known as a *round,* refers to a case that includes powder, primer, and bullet together. One of the triumphs of American firearms manufacture in the nineteenth century was the development of metallic cartridges.

> **FAST FACT**
>
> BB and pellet guns are usually not considered firearms, because they use a burst of air or some other force such as spring operation to fire their projectiles.

Gunpowder and Early Firearms

Gunpowder is an explosive material that burns quickly to form a high-pressure gas. When this gas is released inside the barrel of a gun, it can accelerate a bullet (or anything that will fit in the barrel) to great speed. Gunpowder is the key ingredient needed to construct firearms. Although the Chinese discovered that saltpeter and sulfur could explode as early as the 800s, they were more likely to use gunpowder in fireworks than in weaponry. Arab traders probably passed the knowledge of gunpowder to Europeans by the 1200s.

The inventor of the first firearms is unknown; some of the earliest examples are North African and European cannons used in the 1300s. The Ottoman Turks used gunpowder and huge cannons to batter down the walls of Constantinople (now Istanbul, Turkey) in 1453—walls that had defended the city for almost a thousand years. In the 1400s and 1500s, cannons helped bring down the European social and economic system known as *feudalism.* No longer could powerful nobles feel relatively safe in castles surrounded by high walls, nor did knights on horseback hold all the advantages in battle.

Although the first small firearms appeared in Europe in the 1300s, the *matchlock,* perfected in the late 1400s, was the first effective gun. Matchlocks were cheap to make and easy to repair, but very slow to fire. When a soldier pulled the trigger on a matchlock, a lighted match ignited the gunpowder at the touchhole, a small hole at the breech of the gun—the part behind the barrel—causing the bullet to be fired. However, matchlocks were useless in the rain. These guns were replaced by complicated *wheel locks* in the early 1500s and then by *flintlocks,* perfected around 1635. The flintlock used a striking mechanism of flint-against-steel to produce the spark necessary to fire the powder. European colonists brought flintlocks with them to America. The flintlock ignition system would remain standard for guns until the 1840s.

The earliest firearms were less effective than crossbows, but between 1600 and 1800, guns became a crucial element in European warfare. Europeans then spread firearms across the world wherever they colonized foreign lands. The Spanish, Dutch, British, French, and Swedes who invaded America in the 1600s all used guns in the wars for control of

FAST FACT

At Pavia (in present-day Italy) in 1515, the French and Italians, armed with matchlocks, supposedly postponed their attack on the army of the Holy Roman Emperor because of a torrential downpour. They eventually grew weary of waiting for better weather and went home.

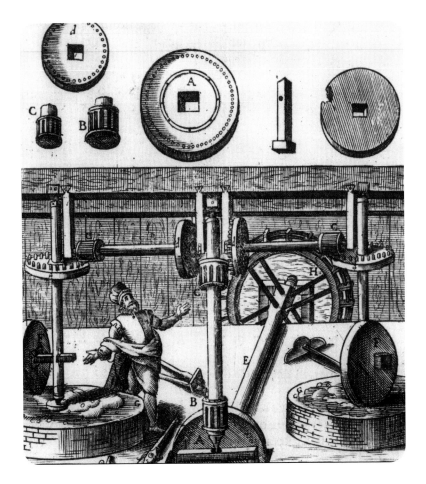

This European engraving from 1656 shows a complex-looking machine used for grinding carbon (an element that makes up coal, petroleum, and other products) into gunpowder.

North America. Many native peoples, such as the Aztecs of Mexico, believed that European firearms had magical powers. In many rebellions against colonial invaders, such as those by the Boxers in China, the Zulu in South Africa, and the "Ghost Dance" Sioux in the United States, native leaders claimed an equally magical ability to bat away bullets or make it impossible for guns to hurt their followers.

Use of Firearms in the United States

The United States currently has one of the highest proportions of gun ownership in the world. Although it's impossible to say for sure, an estimated 70 million Americans own about 200 million to 250 million guns. Of this total, about one-third are handguns, owned by approximately 40 million people.

Americans own guns for many different reasons and often for multiple purposes. Although polling results vary, a typical result indicates that 51 percent of American gun owners own their guns primarily for hunting, 32 percent own them primarily for personal protection, 13 percent own them mainly for target shooting, and 4 percent own them for the sake of collecting. If the questions are restricted to handgun owners, the results come out quite differently: 10 percent own them for hunting, 58 percent own them for personal protection, 18 percent own them for target shooting, and 14 percent own them for collecting. No one generally admits to owning a gun for the sake of attacking other people.

Military Weapons

The U.S. military is obviously one of the major purchasers of firearms in America. The United States has fought many wars in its history, but until 1945 the army was usually quite small in peacetime. American gun manufacturers could and did make good money supplying the military with weapons during wars, but it was an uncertain business, since the army always demobilized after every war, leaving thousands of surplus weapons piled up in armories.

Army National Guardsmen in New Mexico train with an M-16 rifle (left) and a 9mm pistol. Although the U.S. military is a major purchaser of firearms, the M-16, which has needed few updates, has been its primary weapon since the 1960s. Therefore, gun manufacturers make most of their profits from the civilian market.

A mixture of government-owned arsenals and private companies typically supplied the U.S. armed forces; in particular, the Springfield Armory in Massachusetts played a major role in the history of the firearms industry in the United States. The creation of a permanent standing army of enormous size after World War II (1939–1945) has allowed some Defense Department suppliers, such as aerospace manufacturers, to make a fortune. However, this has not been the case for the firearms industry—a couple of fighter jets cost the same as firearms for the entire army. The standard military firearm, the M-16, has set a record by remaining in service for almost forty years without the need for extensive remodeling or replacement. Gun manufacturers continue to make most of their profits from the civilian market.

In the last twenty years, the American firearms industry has been involved in bitter arguments over the role of so-called assault weapons in the civilian market. The definition of an assault weapon is not precise; the assault weapons ban passed by the U.S. Congress in 1994 was a long and complex law that listed nineteen assault-style weapons. Generally, assault firearms are antipersonnel rifles, shotguns, and handguns designed mainly for military and law enforcement purposes. Some general characteristics include the ability to accept a detachable ammunition magazine, flash suppressors, bipod mounts, pistol grips on rifles or shotguns, and threaded barrels allowing for the easy attachment of silencers. These weapons, usually associated with the military, are controversial, because they are only rarely used for self-defense or hunting.

Hunting Weapons

Hunting with weapons dates back beyond the bow and arrow to the boomerang, sling, and spear. Hunting provided food for both Native Americans and the Europeans who invaded the continent in the 1600s and 1700s, although its importance and popularity are disputed. Certainly, trapping and the use of domesticated animals were more reliable and

Hunting has long been a part of life in America. At first it was a way to get food, but over time hunting has evolved into mainly a recreational activity. With hunting lands being lost to development, however, its popularity has declined. These hunters take advantage of the first day of pheasant-hunting season in Kansas.

less time-consuming methods to put meat on the table. For most Americans, hunting was probably always a recreational activity, although it could be an important source of extra income for some farm families. Firearms first came into wide use in hunting in the eighteenth century, and Americans' widespread familiarity with the rifle before 1800 was due to American hunting practices. Rifles were much slower to reload than muskets, but deer and pheasants generally did not shoot back.

In the 1990s, the increasing sprawl caused by the suburbanization of America led to a decline in hunting. A recent survey by the U.S. Fish and Wildlife Service revealed that the typical hunter in 2001 was white, male, and forty-two—older than in the past. Between 1996 and 2001, the number of hunters apparently declined from 14 million to 13 million—a 7 percent decrease. Hunting is most popular among men in rural areas—but rural areas are fast disappearing. In 1991, 22 percent of the American population lived in rural areas but accounted for 46 percent of the nation's hunters; by 2001, the rural population had dropped to 19 percent and made up 41 percent of the nation's hunters. Although some studies by gun groups dispute these findings, the increased disappearance of open land, and the need to travel farther to hunt, have changed the nature of firearms production.

The industry is now less oriented toward participants in shooting sports. Instead, gun manufacturers and dealers appeal to the anxieties of Americans worried about crime and personal self-defense. Handguns are gradually overtaking rifles as the most important and profitable products of the American firearms industry.

Handguns, Crime, and Self-Defense

In the 1950s, handguns represented only about one-fifth of all guns purchased in the United States. Beginning in the late 1960s, however, their sales began to increase dramatically. Until 1967, American handgun sales had never totaled more than 700,000 in any year, yet handgun sales exceeded 2 million every year between 1979 and 1982. From 1982 to 1993, Americans bought 50 million guns, of which about 20 million were handguns. Handguns continue to be the weapon of choice for both self-defense and crime.

Modern American handguns can be divided into revolvers and pistols. *Revolvers* use a round cylinder for the *ammunition magazine,* the container in a firearm that stores the cartridges before they pass into the chamber for firing. In a revolver, the magazine also acts as a chamber when it is lined up with the gun barrel. A shooter cannot use a *single-action revolver* without manually cocking the hammer after each shot. In a *double-action revolver,* the weapon fires each time that the trigger is pulled, and the cylinder then automatically advances to the next chamber. In 1994, Congress passed a law that restricted magazine capacity to ten rounds or less; a revolver's cylinder usually holds six cartridges. Many police forces continue to use revolvers, but semiautomatic pistols are gradually replacing them.

A *pistol* is a handgun with a chamber permanently lined up with the bore. A modern-day pistol is a semiautomatic handgun that carries extra cartridges in a magazine that is usually located in the handle of the handgun, instead of using a revolving cylinder. When the pistol is fired, spring pressure forces a new cartridge from the magazine and automatically loads it in the chamber. Pistols are sometimes known as "automatics" (for their loading), but the term is not really accurate; a pistol requires a separate trigger pull for each shot. Fully automatic pistols fire many cartridges with one trigger pull; these are known as *machine pistols.*

One smaller category of pistols and revolvers is known in the United States as "Saturday night specials" or "junk guns." These are small, short-barreled handguns made of low-quality, cheap materials. Because they are inaccurate except at close range, they have no sporting purpose and are best suited for self-defense or criminal activity. They are the weapons most typically targeted by gun control proponents for government restrictions.

Although handguns are Americans' favorite guns for self-defense, they are also the firearms most frequently used by criminals. The U.S. Department of Justice estimated that in 2001, about 470,000 violent crimes involved handguns in the United States (down from 880,000 in 1993). This does not include approximately 10,000 gun homicides that year. The production of handguns in tremendous numbers remains one of the most controversial aspects of the firearms industry.

The Sport of Shooting Develops

The sport of shooting involves firing at stationary or moving targets with any of a variety of guns: rifles, shotguns, pistols, or revolvers. Distances vary considerably, as do the type of target and even the shooter's position. Competition is usually divided by gender. *Plinking* is the informal shooting of tin cans or objects found at random in the woods; it is probably as popular as formal target shooting. Competitive sport shooting, such as depicted in the famous painting by George Caleb Bingham, dates back to colonial times; it was as likely to be a hobby of wealthy idlers as a sport of backwoodsmen.

In the early 1800s, formal competitive shooting was rare. Occasionally, New York firefighters formed "target companies" that practiced shooting. More important to the development of the sport in America were German immigrants fleeing the failed Revolution of 1848 in Germany. These immigrants formed social organizations known as *Schutzenbunde,* which held festive celebrations featuring uniformed marksmen. The bloody U.S. Civil War (1860–1865) underlined the importance of guns and marksmanship. The National Rifle Association (NRA) was organized two months after the violent New York City "Orange Riot" of 1871 specifically in order to train National Guard regiments how to shoot rifles. Shooting clubs appeared in what became known as the Gilded Age, from 1876 to 1900, scheduling matches and awarding trophies. Wild West shows popularized target shooting and made national celebrities out of sharpshooters such as Frank Butler, Annie Oakley, and William Cody (Buffalo Bill).

The early justification for shooting competitively was its usefulness. The American sport was tied to patriotism,

Sharp-shooting sensation Annie Oakley was born Phoebe Anne Oakley Mosee in Ohio in 1860. She was part of Buffalo Bill's traveling Wild West show from 1885 to 1902. Her amazing shooting talent helped to popularize sport shooting at the end of the nineteenth century.

nationalism, and character building. Control and repetition were (and remain) essential parts of target shooting; riflery required so much discipline that it barely seemed like recreation. A hunting magazine stated in 1875, "Rifle practice carries with it self-denial, sobriety, and iron nerve." The popularity of marksmanship in the U.S. Army in the 1890s inspired a shooting craze in America in the early 1900s. The firearms industry did its best to sponsor all these activities, seeing in the rise of shooting sports an easy market for increased sales of guns.

Trapshooting, Skeet, and the Olympics

Trapshooting involves firing at clay targets hurled into the air by a mechanical spring "trap." The sport began in Great Britain in the 1800s and first became popular in the United States in the 1880s. Modern participants now shoot at saucers made of silt and pitch from a distance between 16 and 25 yards (14.5 and 22.5 meters). The American Trapshooting Association formed in 1900 and changed its name to the Amateur Trapshooting Association (ATA) in 1923. It holds an annual championship in Vandalia, Ohio, although there has been much discussion about relocating it in recent years. The ATA claims more than 50,000 members who participate in 6,000 registered tournaments throughout North America. In 1998, 1,300 gun clubs associated with the ATA threw more than 80 million clay targets.

Skeet is a form of trapshooting in which clay targets are used to imitate birds in flight. C.E. Davies, Henry W. Davies, and William Foster originated the sport in 1920 at Glen Rock Kennels in Andover, Massachusetts. These men took turns firing at clay targets, and their shooting gradually developed into a regular program with a uniform series of shots to keep the competition fair. The name "skeet" was chosen in a contest in the February 1926 issues of *National Sportsman* and *Hunting and Fishing* magazines. Almost 10,000 entries were received when a prize of $100 was offered for the best name for the new sport. The judges settled on *skeet,* an old Scandinavian form of the word "shoot." The National Skeet Shooting Association, the main American organization, boasts nearly 20,000 members.

Shooting events have been part of the modern summer Olympic Games since they started in 1896. Popular Olympic events include pistol shooting at 50 meters (55 yards), rifle shooting at 300 meters (330 yards), trapshooting, skeet, and small-bore rifle shooting. Until 1979, there was no year-round U.S. Shooting Team. Shooters trained on their own and met once a year to try out for major events such as the Olympics and World Championships. Once the match was over, the team disbanded until the following year. In 1985, a $2.7 million Olympic Shooting Center was completed in Colorado Springs, Colorado. It is the largest indoor shooting facility in the United States, with three separate shooting ranges. The most prolific medal winner in Olympic shooting was Carl T. Osburn of the United States. He won five gold, four silver, and two bronze medals in the 1912, 1920, and 1924 Olympics.

> **FAST FACT**
>
> In the *biathlon*, cross-country skiers, racing across a hilly course, stop to shoot at fixed targets with rifles. Originally a Swedish hunting competition, it became a regular feature of the winter Olympic Games beginning in 1960.

Collectors

Americans are collectors; 60 percent of U.S. households own collectibles. Firearms are perfect for collecting. There are guns to suit almost every budget and they have widespread appeal for the mechanically minded, the history buff, and the person who admires beautiful workmanship. The long and romantic history of the American firearms industry and its ties to patriotism make collecting historic firearms, and even acquiring imitations and commemorative firearms, an exceedingly popular hobby with several hundred thousand gun collectors.

As in many forms of collecting, the value of a historic firearm depends almost entirely on its condition. Other than "new" (in the original box) and "perfect" (new, but not in the original box), all other classifications are completely subjective and subject to loud argument. Most firearms do not have good investment potential; they're collected more for the love of guns than for the opportunity to make money. Some firearms, however, can be extraordinarily valuable. One of the most expensive guns ever sold was an 1873 .45-caliber Colt army revolver, Serial No. 1. On May 14, 1987, it was sold at auction in New York City for $242,000.

The bulk of the buying and selling of collectors' guns is done at gun shows, and the so-called gun-show loophole has become a major issue in the debate over firearms in the United States. The Brady Handgun Violence Protection Act, passed by the U.S. Congress in 1993, required only licensed gun dealers to perform background checks on customers purchasing firearms. But in most states, anyone can buy a gun, without undergoing a background check, from an unlicensed seller at a gun show. More than 4,000 gun shows are held in the United States every year, and an estimated 40 percent of gun sales occur at venues such as gun shows or flea markets. The firearms industry benefits from gun shows, which serve as a major way to distribute firearms in the United States. However, the industry dreads incidents such as the Columbine High School massacre in Littleton, Colorado, in 1999. In this deadly school shooting, three of the four guns were acquired at a gun show in 1998. At the time, a high school senior bought the guns for the murderers, who were then seventeen and too young to purchase the weapons by themselves. As with many other issues concerning guns, firearms manufacturers were caught between the desire to sell their product and the fallout from its misuse.

Guns—A Symbol of America

Firearms play a crucial role in American culture, whether they are used for military purposes, hunting, self-defense, crime, sports, or as collectibles. The minuteman, the frontiersman, the cowboy, the gangster, the marine, and the police officer are all international symbols of America, spread by the mass media throughout the country and the world. All are associated to some degree with the possession of guns. For good or ill, the importance of the manufacture of firearms cannot be denied.

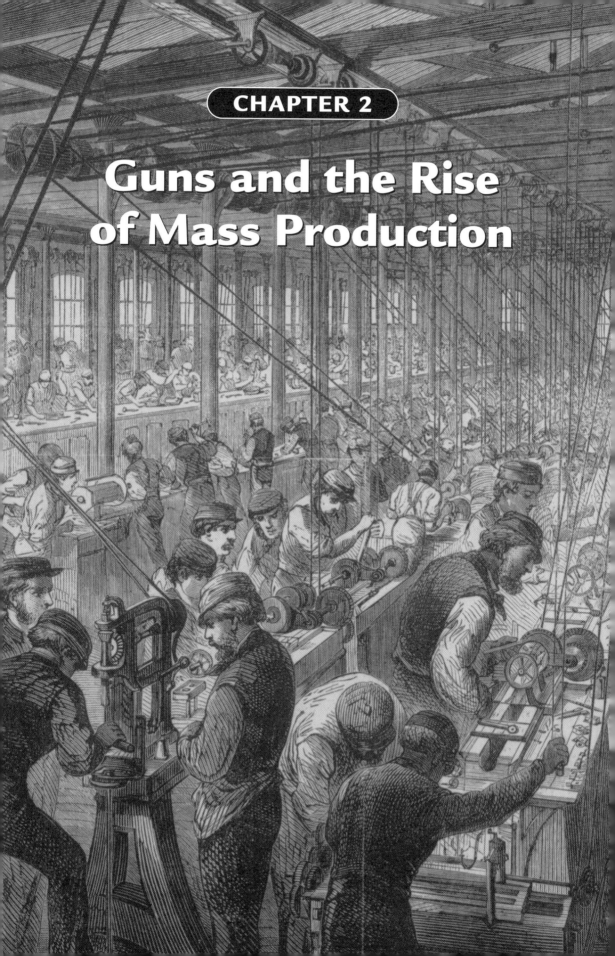

CHAPTER 2

Guns and the Rise of Mass Production

The major inventions that began the world's Industrial Revolution were created in Great Britain in the 1700s. Americans in 1800 were technically backward compared to their former colonial masters. Yet by the end of the century, the United States firearms industry had revolutionized the way that things were manufactured. By the mid-1800s, some people were already calling this new way "the American system of manufacturing."

This system involved many noteworthy changes. Most importantly, factories brought together under a single roof separate manufacturing processes that used to be performed in people's homes or small shops. The manufacturing of a product was broken into small steps (*division of labor*), and machines were invented specifically for each step. All workers became subject to the same work standards. Instead of learning a craft as an apprentice, then a journeyman, and finally a master, workers now became employees, performing unskilled tasks over and over again. Precision machinery slowly replaced hand tools; the parts of mass-produced objects became uniform through the use of careful gauges and quality control.

These changes occurred throughout the world to some degree; the system of interchangeable parts had forerunners in Russia, Great Britain, and especially France. Yet the American arms industry in particular pioneered these developments, and they became so closely related to the manufacture of weapons in the United States that in 1854 the British government sent a parliamentary commission to tour America and report on American firearms production.

The new era of machine-oriented mass production was specifically tied to gun production because of the needs of armies in the 1800s. Beginning in the late 1700s, European governments had begun to rely on enormous armies of draftees serving for short periods of time. Napoleon invaded Russia in 1812 with a gargantuan army of 614,000 soldiers; he was opposed by 400,000 Russians. Obviously, governments needed huge amounts of weapons, raw materials, and skilled workers to supply armies of this size. The production of weapons in immense quantities would turn the mass army into an incredibly destructive force. Although such enormous armies would not be seen in the United States until the Civil War, the War Department realized as early as 1800 that it would need to acquire weapons in much greater numbers than a local village gunsmith could provide.

The Role of the Federal Government

It takes a great deal of money to manufacture and sell firearms in large quantities. Before a single gun can be produced, money must be spent on materials, tools, shop facilities, and skilled laborers. In the early transition to mass production, many of the largest arms makers in the United States depended almost entirely on the federal government. These arms makers would sign contracts with the U.S. government and then use the large cash advances to produce weapons. The government payment was often an early gun maker's only source of capital.

For example, when Eli Whitney signed a contract in 1798 to produce 10,000 muskets for the government, he used the generous federal payments to build a factory, pay off his own personal debt, and fight lawsuits over his cotton gin. In the early 1800s, the United States depended on private armorers such as Whitney, Asa Waters, and Simeon North for advances in technology, but the inventors often relied on public money through government subsidy for patronage.

The Need for an Armory

The years leading to the American Revolution (1775–1783) had demonstrated the importance of firearms and the need to find a safe place to store them. The battles at Lexington and Concord that had begun the Revolution had been triggered by the British search for the colonists' weapons. In 1777, General George Washington and his chief of artillery, Henry Knox, selected Springfield, Massachusetts, as a safe and centrally located place to store muskets and cannons away from the British. The government also owned and operated magazines (to store weapons and powder) at Philadelphia and Carlisle, Pennsylvania and West Point, New York.

After the war, the new American government under the Articles of Confederation kept the Springfield arsenal open. In 1786 and 1787, the weapons stored here attracted the attention of Daniel Shays and other poor farmers in the incident known as Shays's Rebellion. This uprising led many wealthier people to fear for the security of their private property and to call for a new constitutional convention to produce a stronger central government. In that way, the arsenal at Springfield played a crucial role in the creation of the U.S. Constitution.

America had traditionally produced few of its own weapons for its soldiers; during the Revolution, the rebels had imported almost 80,000 French muskets. In the 1790s, the newly formed United States faced an uncertain political situation. War with either Great Britain or France seemed extremely likely. The young government

Massachusetts native Henry Knox was a general under George Washington during the Revolutionary War. When Washington became the first president of the United States, Knox was named secretary of war. Knox played a key role in establishing the arsenal at Springfield and in making it one of only two national arsenals in the country.

purchased some weapons from importers who received them across an Atlantic Ocean dominated by potentially hostile European navies. Other weapons were purchased from private contractors who were notoriously corrupt and deceived the government on every possible occasion.

The first U.S. president, General George Washington, had learned firsthand in the American Revolution how the lack of firearms could cripple an army's ability to fight. He was determined that the U.S. government should manufacture its own muskets. He sponsored a bill, which Congress approved in April 1794, "for the erecting and repairing of Arsenals and Magazines." This legislation allotted $81,000 for the establishment of up to four national arsenals and gave the president the right to pick the locations. Springfield, sponsored by Secretary of War Henry Knox, a native Massachusetts resident, was an obvious choice. With the rest of the money, Washington decided to construct one new, large arsenal rather than rebuild the Revolutionary War magazines already owned by the government. Against the advice of his military engineer and two secretaries of war, Washington chose a remote location at Harpers Ferry, Virginia, as the site for the second U.S. arsenal. Perhaps intentionally, Washington had placed one arsenal in the North and one in the South.

Simeon North and the Beginnings of Mass Production

In 1798, the United States teetered on the brink of war with France. The creation of the two federal arsenals did not mean that the government could not also work through private production. When the U.S. War Department feared that it did not have enough weapons, it began issuing cash-advance contracts with private manufacturers for muskets and pistols. Simeon North, a manufacturer of agricultural equipment, and Eli Whitney, the famed inventor of the cotton gin, were among the first to sign these contracts. Both were extremely interested in the idea of producing interchangeable parts.

FAST FACT

The words *armory* and *arsenal* are often considered synonyms today, but in the eighteenth and nineteenth centuries, the words had very specific, separate meanings. An *armory* was a place where arms were manufactured, while an *arsenal* was a place for storing all sorts of war supplies, including weapons. A *magazine* served as a storehouse for gunpowder and ammunition. Some places, such as Springfield, Massachusetts, filled all of these functions at one time or another.

Although Whitney did a better job at publicizing himself, North was more successful at using a division of labor to actually produce interchangeable parts. In October 1798, the U.S. government signed a contract with North for 500 horse pistols to be delivered within one year; in 1800, he received another contract for an additional 1,500 pistols. North found that by "confining a workman to one particular limb of the pistol until he has made nearly two thousand, I save at least one quarter of his labor." North was one of the first manufacturers to break gun production into separate procedures, a technique absolutely crucial to mass production.

North developed many other improvements in arms making, especially the use of newly invented (sometimes by him) special-purpose machinery to produce weapons. In 1813, in the midst of the War of 1812 (1812–1815), North signed a contract with the War Department for 20,000 more pistols. The contract specifically stated, "The component parts of pistols are to correspond so exactly that any limb or part of one Pistol may be fitted to any other Pistol of the twenty thousand." No previous War Department contract had ever contained this type of wording.

In 1816, North had to ask for an additional $50,000 to fulfill the contract, and the secretary of war ordered an investigation. The superintendents of the Springfield and Harpers Ferry armories visited North's factory in Berlin, Connecticut, and were astounded by what they saw. They not only agreed that North was entirely capable of fulfilling the contract and gave him the money that he had requested, but they also admitted that he had obtained a uniformity of parts unknown at the federal armories. If anyone can claim to be the father of American mass production, it is probably Simeon North.

North was not the only innovator in firearms manufacture. In 1808, Asa Waters's factory in Millbury, Massachusetts, adapted the idea of using groove-faced trip-hammers to forge iron bars into gun barrels. The heavy, regulated blows of the water-powered hammers

produced a much sounder seam in half the time needed to weld a barrel by hand; the trip-hammers also cut labor costs markedly. The technology rapidly spread to Springfield and throughout the arms industry.

The Role of Eli Whitney

Eli Whitney had acquired large debts from trying to defend his claim that he had invented the cotton gin (he received a patent in 1794), as well as from his failure to produce cotton gins profitably at his factory in New Haven, Connecticut. With the help of the secretary of the treasury, fellow Yale graduate Oliver Wolcott, Whitney became the first private citizen to receive a cash advance from the U.S. government for a manufacturing contract in 1798. He promised to produce a phenomenal 10,000 muskets within the next twenty-eight months. In exchange, he would be paid $134,000, or $13.40 a musket—a few dollars more than the going rate for imported firearms. This War Department contract was one of the first ever made for a mass-produced item. More importantly for Whitney, he admitted that the contract "saved me from ruin."

Whitney had no experience making guns. To a degree, however, this was also an advantage, because he had no attachment to the craft or to the artistic value of a unique

This is one of the 500 pistols manufactured for the United States government by Simeon North at his Connecticut factory in 1798–1799. Over the next few decades, North fulfilled several more contracts with the government, which was very impressed with North's mass production techniques.

Eli Whitney's friendship with Secretary of the Treasury Oliver Wolcott helped Whitney secure a government contract in 1798 to manufacture 10,000 muskets in a little over two years. The government paid its first-ever cash advance to Whitney, who sorely needed the money. Whitney is pictured here in 1815.

gun. Whitney dreamed of manufacturing guns in which every part of each firearm was interchangeable. He wrote to Wolcott that he would "form the tool so that the tools themselves shall fashion the work and give to every part its just proportion—which when accomplished will give...uniformity, and exactness to the whole." Whitney believed that machines in America would have "to substitute for that skill of the artist which is acquired only by long practice and experience; a species of skill which is not possessed in this country to any considerable extent." The use of machines would be crucial, since even a government institution such as the Springfield Armory had never yet produced 5,000 muskets in its best year.

After twenty-eight months, not a single musket had been completed, while Whitney spent most of his time in the South arguing lawsuits regarding the cotton gin. In 1801, desperate for more money, Whitney gave a dramatic demonstration that proved to President John Adams, Vice President (and President-elect) Thomas Jefferson, and members of the cabinet that his "interchangeable system" really worked. For the astounded onlookers, Whitney assembled ten different locks to the same musket. Although he interchanged only the assembled locks, Jefferson took the bait and believed that Whitney was making interchangeable lock parts. The Jefferson administration gave him even more money and more time, and Whitney finally completed his contract. He delivered the last musket in January 1809, ten years after the date of the initial agreement.

Although Whitney was eight years late, he notably linked firearms manufacture and machine production. He also helped popularize the idea of interchangeable parts, even if he never quite developed the means to make the idea work. Nonetheless, Whitney, who never received any large sums of money from the cotton gin, continued promoting mass production in arms making until his death in 1825.

John H. Hall and the Harpers Ferry Armory

The armory at Harpers Ferry began producing muskets around 1800; by 1816, it was turning out nearly 10,000 arms a year. Under the leadership of Superintendent James Stubblefield from 1815 to 1829, this armory became a major contributor to the development of modern production methods. The chief innovator was John H. Hall, originally a Maine cabinetmaker and boatbuilder.

Hall's goal was to produce a *breech-loading rifle* with interchangeable parts. (A breechloader loads bullets into the barrel at the trigger end of the gun. This allows the shooter to avoid having to put the bullets in at the end the barrel and then use a ramrod to stuff them down into the gun.) Hall patented a breech-loading rifle in 1811 and received his first order from the government for 100 of them in 1817. The breech-loading rifle was a relative success, and the War Department hired Hall in 1819 to produce 1,000 rifles at Harpers Ferry for a monthly salary of sixty dollars and a royalty of a dollar per gun.

The U.S. government paid the full cost of manufacturing the guns, thereby completely supporting Hall's financial needs without paying out cash advances, like those that had been given to Whitney and North. Hall was now a kind of private manufacturer at a public armory. In his twenty years at Harpers Ferry, the Yankee inventor developed new metal- and woodworking machinery, as well as constructing and improving drop hammers, drilling machines, stock-making machines (to shape the handles of guns), and machines to perform a variety of specialized cutting actions.

Hall also extensively used precision gauges and measuring devices to standardize production and make sure that all parts came out the same. When he finally completed the contract in December 1824, the breech-loading rifle parts really did interchange. Hall proudly wrote to Secretary of War John Calhoun,

> I have succeeded in an object which had hitherto completely baffled...those who have heretofore attempted it—I have succeeded in establishing methods for fabricating arms exactly alike, & with economy, by the hands of common workmen, & in such a manner as to endure a perfect observance of any established model.

A committee established by the House of Representatives confirmed all of Hall's claims in 1827.

Hall's breechloaders were popular with many state militias, but it was illegal for federal arms factories to produce weapons for the states. In 1828, the War Department gave Simeon North a five-year contract to produce 5,000 Hall-type breechloaders. By using Hall's models and gauges, Harpers Ferry and North's armory in Connecticut eventually turned out rifles that had nearly identical parts. This was a highlight in the history of firearms manufacturing; for the first time, two widely separated arms factories were producing fully interchangeable weapons.

The Springfield Armory

In 1832, the Harpers Ferry Armory was the equal of Springfield when it came to innovation in firearms production. Colonel George Talcott wrote in 1832 that

"Hall's manufactory has been carried out to a greater degree of perfection, as regards the quality of the work and uniformity of parts than is to be found anywhere—almost everything is performed by machinery, leaving very little dependent on manual labor." After this date, however, the initiative drifted to Northern arms makers and entrepreneurs in the Connecticut River valley, especially those near the armory at Springfield.

When it was founded in 1794, the Springfield Armory made muskets almost entirely by hand, using the skills developed by generations of gunsmiths. Yet within fifty years, the armory would become a world leader in the manufacture of firearms and a center for invention and development. It began to prosper with the arrival of

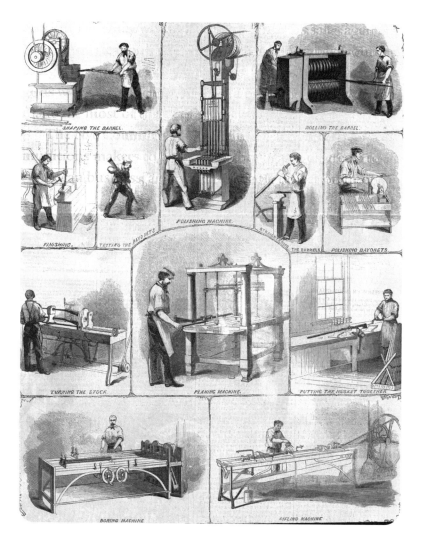

This print shows scenes of gun manufacture at the Springfield Armory, which was in operation from 1794 to 1968. In the early nineteenth century, Springfield, along with its counterpart in Harpers Ferry, Virginia, became a world center for developing gun technology.

Superintendent Colonel Roswell Lee, who served from 1815 to his death in 1833. Lee was a great supporter of new machine technology and the goal of interchangeable firearm parts. More importantly, he believed in cooperation between the armory and private arms makers to take advantage of the armory's location in a region filled with foundries, machine shops, mills, and skilled labor.

It was at Springfield that Thomas Blanchard invented a lathe for making gun stocks; Erskine Allin introduced the "Allin Conversion," which converted outdated muzzleloaders into breechloaders; and John Garand invented the M-1 semiautomatic rifle. The armory produced many famous American small arms, including the Model 1855 rifle-musket used in the Civil War, the famous 1873 Springfield "trapdoor" rifle, and the Model 1903 used in World War I (1914–1918). In the 1890s, the armory became the U.S. Army's main laboratory for the development and testing of new small arms, which became Springfield's primary responsibility after the end of World War II (1939–1945).

> **FAST FACT**
>
> The Department of Defense closed the Springfield Armory in 1968. The 55-acre (22-hectare) armory is now a National Historic Site, containing many surviving nineteenth-century buildings and one of the world's largest collections of small arms.

The Department of Ordnance

In June 1812, Congress voted to declare war against Great Britain, the strongest nation in the world at that time. The U.S. Army Ordnance Department, newly created that year, was given the responsibility of arming American soldiers and inspecting military supplies. Under the able leadership of Decius Wadsworth, the Ordnance Department expanded the number of arsenals that would manufacture weaponry: Georgetown, Virginia, would produce cannon; Pittsburgh, Pennsylvania, would produce gun carriages; and Watervliet, on the Hudson River across from Troy, New York, would produce small articles of equipment.

In February 1815, at the close of the near-disastrous War of 1812, Secretary of War James Monroe convinced Congress to give complete control of the national armories to the new Ordnance Department. The army, after its experience in the War of 1812, believed that many of the thousands of weapons that had been damaged in the field could have been repaired if parts had been interchangeable. Under Wadsworth, the Ordnance Department led the movement to introduce uniform standards into weapon construction—at the very least between the national armories at Springfield and Harpers Ferry. The government also encouraged a national arms industry by favoring the contracting of American gun makers for complete weapons. Until the 1840s, the U.S. Army did not worry about the high cost of weapons. Instead, the military tried to persuade arms manufacturers to stop following traditional gunsmithing procedures and switch to machine production in order to deliver higher-quality weapons.

> **FAST FACT**
>
> The Watervliet Arsenal, founded in 1813, is America's oldest continually active arsenal. In 2003, it was still government-owned, government-operated, and manufacturing artillery for the U.S. Army.

The Use of Gauges and Blanchard's Lathe

For hundreds of years, individual artisans had slowly and skillfully made the component parts of guns (locks, mountings, stocks, and barrels). A gun lock is the part of the gun that fires the bullet or cartridge. Making them was particularly tricky. They required careful forging, grinding, filing, and finishing. Gun barrels were also difficult to make and often failed even a visual inspection. In the end, gun parts had to be carefully fitted together; attaching the lock and barrel to the gun stock was a slow and costly job. Gun making was an art passed from master to apprentice during a long period of training. The gunsmith often made the entire object; the work was not just a job but part of an entire way of life.

In 1817, urged on by the Ordnance Department, Roswell Lee began experimenting with inspection gauges to ensure the uniformity of parts. Before this time, inspection was simply done by looking at the firearms. In 1822, the War Department established specific regulations for the inspection of finished firearms. These new developments implied that gun parts needed to be uniform, if not interchangeable.

The production of gun stocks was not divided or mechanized until 1819. In that year, Thomas Blanchard, a local mechanic working at the Springfield Armory, invented a special lathe that allowed a worker to quickly and easily produce identical irregular shapes such as gun stocks, ax handles, and shoe lasts. In addition to his patented lathe, Blanchard designed fourteen other different woodworking machines that almost completely eliminated hand labor in stock making. Blanchard's procedure became the basic principle of machine production in American manufacturing: a sequence of different machines, each designed to carry out one operation, was arranged in a specific order to perform all the necessary steps required to complete a manufacturing task.

From 1830 until the Civil War, Springfield led the way in the development of interchangeable parts for firearms. New machine tools invented by armorers Thomas Warner and Cyrus Buckland allowed a musket to be manufactured almost entirely by machine (except for the barrel welding). By 1850, the parts of each individual firearm lock were so similar that the armory no longer fitted, assembled, and marked the lock parts in the soft state before hardening them. The Springfield Armory had achieved almost complete interchangeability in the parts of its muskets.

New developments at Springfield quickly passed through the firearms manufacturing field. The armory

This lathe, invented by Sylvester Nash at the Springfield Armory in 1817, predated Thomas Blanchard's lathe by two years. However, Nash's lathe was unable to form the shape at the butt end of a gun's barrel, so it did not gain the recognition of Blanchard's, which did achieve the required shape.

trained many mechanics who later worked for other arms makers or manufacturers. Private and federal armories exchanged parts, workers, and information about production machinery. Springfield frequently transferred men and machinery to Harpers Ferry and to nearby private firms to spread new production techniques.

Other developments also modernized production. The rapid adoption of metal- and wood-shaping tools put the firearms industry far ahead of other branches of manufacturing and provided opportunities for numerous skilled, technically proficient workers. The machine tool industry developed in the 1850s in response to demands from firearms manufacturers. Mechanics in the machine tool industry spread the new technology to other metalworking businesses, such as the manufacture of sewing machines, hardware, agricultural machinery, and railway equipment. Factories began to measure the individual production of each worker by the job; sometimes, bosses even paid "piecework," meaning the worker's pay depended on the output.

> **FAST FACT**
>
> Thomas Blanchard was one of the most celebrated inventors of the 1800s. Besides his lathe, he also invented an apple parer, machines to produce tacks, a machine to cut and fold envelopes, and a method for bending large pieces of wood.

The Rise of Patent Arms

In the 1840s, American government contracts with private arms makers for military weapons declined and older weapons supply companies, such as those operated by Simeon North and Asa Waters, began to disappear. A new type of firearms manufacturer replaced them—makers of *patent arms,* such as the Sharps rifle or the Colt revolver. These firms took advantage of the new technology so carefully fostered at the government-sponsored armories and used it to efficiently manufacture firearms at a considerable profit. Only companies with deep financial resources, such as Colt and Remington, could afford to buy the new machines necessary to meet the requirements of the contracts issued by the Ordnance Department.

For example, in 1845, the small shop of gun makers Samuel Robbins and Richard Lawrence (and, originally, Nicanor Kendall) was awarded a government contract for

10,000 rifles with interchangeable parts. Their bid of
$10.90 per rifle was ten cents lower than any competing
bid. Although the company had only twenty-five workers
at the time, Robbins & Lawrence promptly hired a
hundred more and built a modern armory. They stocked it
with the newest technology, such as the turret lathe and an
improved line of drilling, milling, and planing machines.
Unbelievably, Robbins & Lawrence came in eighteen
months ahead of deadline, producing high-quality rifles at
a profit. The small firm won international acclaim for its
firearms at the Crystal Palace Exhibition in 1851—a sort of
industrial world's fair in London, England. Unfortunately,
despite their success, Robbins & Lawrence had
overexpanded. Without great financial resources,
the company was bankrupt by 1859.

The Colt Armory

Samuel Colt, an American inventor and entrepreneur,
patented his breech-loading revolving pistol in 1835 and
1836. There did not appear to be any market for the
weapon until the U.S. government ordered 1,000 revolvers
during the Mexican War (1846–1848). The contract
specifically stated that the revolver locks had to be "made
of the best cast or double sheet steel and the parts
sufficiently uniform to be interchanged with slight or no
refitting." The government merely purchased Colt's
revolvers; it did not give him any models from its own
armories or offer him any cash advance. Almost half of
Colt's production did not meet government standards,
but he discovered, to his surprise, that the general public
would pay a higher price for the rejected revolvers than he
received from the War Department for first-class weapons.
Colt's revolver was a huge success, and he quickly became
one of the largest manufacturers in the United States.

Colt's belief in the necessity of machine production was
even greater than that of the management at the Springfield
Armory. "With hand labor," Colt said in 1851, "it is not
possible to obtain that amount of uniformity, or accuracy,

The revolvers made by Samuel Colt that were purchased by the U.S. government for use in the Mexican War (1846–1848) were not up to government standards, but this hardly mattered to Colt once he discovered that civilians would pay top dollar for them. Colt is pictured around 1850.

in the several parts, which is so desirable." In 1848, Colt began to manufacture guns in Hartford, Connecticut, and he opened the largest and most modern private armory of the world there in 1855. He used machines to produce large quantities of guns, which drove down the cost of the weapons; this is known as *economy of scale.* Colt supposedly employed the astounding total of 1,100 workers at his Hartford factory, and as many as 1,400 during the Civil War.

The Colt armory became a Hartford institution and huge tourist attraction. Mark Twain visited in 1868 and described

a dense wilderness of strange iron machines that stretches away into remote distances and

FAST FACT

Although tens of thousands of men worked in Colt's armory, not one worker's account has ever been found. It's difficult to say if his employees liked him, enjoyed working there, or despised being machine tenders in the new industrial age.

confusing perspectives—a tangled forest of rods, bars, pulleys, wheels, and all the imaginable and unimaginable form of mechanism...[no] two machines [are] alike, or designed to perform the same office. It must have required more brains to invent all these things than would serve to stock fifty Senates like ours.

With the help of master mechanic Elisha Root, Colt produced 24,000 pistols in 1856, 39,000 in 1857, and 136,000 in 1863 (at the height of the Civil War). In 1853, Colt opened an armory in London, showing off American mass-production, machine-oriented, firearms-making techniques. He assured the British that "there is nothing that cannot be produced by machinery." By the time of Colt's death in 1862, his firm had made and sold almost 1 million guns.

Colt, like many successful entrepreneurs, was an opportunistic master of self-promotion. He brilliantly used newspapers, advertising, testimonials, broadsides (posters), and promotional tours to tout his product. While chasing military contracts and favorable patent rulings, he bribed politicians, military officers, and European nobility with money and expensive weaponry. He referred to himself as Colonel Colt, although he had never served in the army. He continued to imply that his gun parts were interchangeable when tests showed that this claim was not accurate. He did not particularly care where his guns ended up, as long as someone bought them; while the United States hovered on the brink of the Civil War in 1860, Colt sold $61,000 worth of weapons (more than $3 million in today's money) to Alabama, Georgia, Virginia, and Mississippi. He even fired workers who supported *abolitionism,* or abolishing slavery. Nonetheless, Colt was a real innovator in creating a new system of manufacture based on machines and mass production, and he worked ceaselessly and creatively to find or invent new markets for his guns.

The Committee on the Machinery of the United States

The British were astounded by the high quality of American products displayed in London in 1851 at the Crystal Palace Exhibition—especially the American firearms. On the brink of the Crimean War (1853–1856), the British government appointed a Committee on the Machinery of the United States to tour America to investigate and report on the technological revolution in machine-based manufacture. The British were particularly interested in its potential use for the new Royal Small Arms Manufactory in Enfield, England. The British committee toured arms factories, machine shops, and iron foundries from Harpers Ferry to the Mohawk Valley of New York (along the Erie Canal). The committee members paid special attention to the Connecticut River valley, where they visited the Springfield Armory, four major private arms factories, and a handful of machine shops.

According to its report of 1855, the British committee was impressed by the cleverness of American inventors from the Northern states. One visitor commented on the "common-sense way of going to the point at once…there is great simplicity…. no ornamentation, no rubbing away of corners or polishing; but the precise, accurate and correct results." The British commission singled out

> the two national armories of Springfield and Harpers Ferry, the private establishments of Colonel Colt, Robbins, and Lawrence, and the Sharpe's Rifle Company, [which] are all conducted on the thorough manufacturing system, with machinery and special tools applied to the several parts…. Besides the machinery and tools…there are hundreds of valuable instruments and gauges that are employed…the object of all being to secure thorough identity in all parts.

The British commission concluded, "If the military gunmakers of England are wise in their generation, they will not despise this system of manufacture, but on the contrary, will adopt it for it will secure for them a high vantage ground in competing with other parts of the world."

The American System of Manufacturing

The so-called American system of manufacturing combined the idea that machines could make things better and faster than humans with the concept of interchangeable parts. Almost no one, however, referred to firearms manufacture by this phrase at the time; in fact, the term "American system" was rarely used before 1900. Nonetheless, the American firearms industry pioneered the idea of manufacturing a product using a series of operations carried out by special-purpose machines that produce interchangeable parts.

In 1800, a gun would have been made by a single highly skilled artisan (or perhaps several) who had trained for years. Each gun was a handcrafted object; if it broke, it needed to be returned to its maker or another competent gunsmith who could shape and fit a unique replacement piece. The new system, however, made craft almost irrelevant. Unskilled workers who lacked the ability to make an entire gun now manufactured gun parts in large quantities with the help of complex machinery. The thousands of copies of each part were almost identical—close enough so that almost any one could serve as a replacement part in another weapon. If a piece broke, another could be substituted without any craft work such as shaping.

The use of specific machinery and interchangeable parts was one of the greatest contributions of the United States to world technology in the nineteenth century. With this technology, the American firearms industry completely changed the nature of manufacturing in the world and helped speed along the Industrial Revolution.

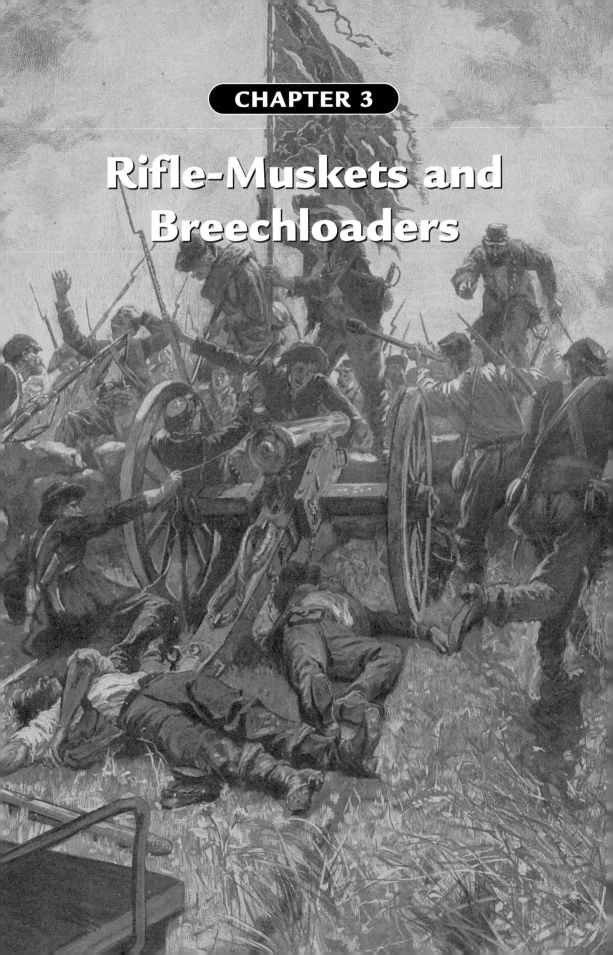

CHAPTER 3

Rifle-Muskets and Breechloaders

At the time of the American Revolution, flintlocks had existed for almost two centuries, and there was no particular reason to think that they wouldn't still be used two centuries in the future. Yet in the 1800s, and particularly in the United States between 1810 and 1870, numerous inventions and technical advances modernized weapons almost beyond recognition. The result was a huge increase in firepower and a radical change in the way that wars were fought. Developments in the American firearms industry had a massive effect on military history; morale, training, discipline, and spirit would all retain some value but would pale compared to the necessities of sheer firepower.

Major nineteenth-century developments in small arms included a rifled bore, breech-loading, and metallic cartridges. These concepts had been known for centuries, but their widespread adoption was often beyond the technology of the day. Breech-loading guns had first been used in the early 1500s, but such weapons could not be effective until better metalworking could produce an airtight breech (that wouldn't let gases escape) and a properly fitted cartridge. The British soldier of the American Revolution and the Napoleonic Wars (1799–1815) in Europe fought with a smoothbore, muzzle-loading, flintlock musket with a bayonet; known as the Short Land Pattern, the musket was later immortalized as "Brown Bess."

The "Kentucky" Rifle

Any projectile travels more accurately if it is spinning. This is the principle behind the rifle, a gun with a rifled (or grooved) barrel. When the gun is fired, the rifling—which runs in a spiral along the barrel's inside—gives the bullet a spinning motion, causing it to almost drill through the air. The spin prevents the bullet from wobbling in flight and makes the weapon far more accurate, with a longer range, than the smoothbore musket.

Rifles date back to the 1400s, but it was expensive to manufacture a rifled barrel, and the gun was very slow to

Having a photographic portrait made was a rare event in 1855. Obviously, this man felt that his portrait would be incomplete unless he posed dramatically with his rifle. This unusual picture offers a good look at a nineteenth-century rifle.

fire. Bullets large enough to fit the rifled barrel sometimes had to be pounded down with a *mallet* (a type of hammer) and a *ramrod* (a rod for ramming down the bullet and the charge). After a rifle had been fired a few times, leftover gunpowder would build up in the grooves and had to be cleaned out before the gun could be used again. In large-scale engagements, the superior accuracy of the rifle was canceled out by the dense cloud of smoke from the gunpowder that hovered over battlefields. Until the 1800s, rifles were almost never used by European armies, which preferred to arm their soldiers with smoothbore muskets.

In America, however, the rifle was often used for hunting, where a single accurate shot might bring down a deer without the danger of the hunter being shot while trying to reload. Some immigrants to Pennsylvania in the 1700s had brought with them the heavy hunting rifle, known as the *jaeger,* used in southern Switzerland and Germany. English settlers used a long-barreled *fowling piece,* a smoothbore that was not particularly accurate. In Pennsylvania around 1725, Swiss and German gunsmiths with mechanical backgrounds and crafts experience began designing and building a "Pennsylvania rifle" adapted to American conditions. This rifle, later misnamed the Kentucky rifle, was probably first developed in Lancaster by Swiss gunsmith Martin Meylin. The new design quickly spread throughout the area and was known as a distinct weapon by 1760.

The Pennsylvania rifle was 42 to 46 inches (106 to 116 centimeters)—longer, more slender, and with a smaller bore (a caliber of about .50) than heavier and less accurate models produced in Europe. Using a ball weighing only about 0.5 ounces (14 grams), the Pennsylvania rifle was also more accurate, supposedly to almost 300 yards (270 meters). Technically, Americans used a short iron rod, a ramrod, and a mallet to reload, but they found this procedure too slow. Instead, they developed a quicker and easier method, using a *patch*—a small greased cloth around a lead ball that could be pushed smoothly down the barrel and produced a tight fit. In a sharp fight at close range, riflemen sometimes discarded their patches completely and rammed the balls down naked. This made the weapon even less accurate than a musket, but fortunately for them, Americans did not often fight at close range.

Compared to European models, American rifles were light and accurate and became the weapons of choice in the backwoods of Kentucky after the French and Indian War (1754–1763). An Anglican minister wrote from Maryland in 1775, "Rifles, infinitely better than those imported, are daily made in many places in Pennsylvania and all the gunsmiths everywhere constantly employed."

Firearms and Military Tactics Around 1800

European armies of the early 1800s designed their tactics around the smoothbore musket. A well-trained soldier, if he had mastered the twelve-step process, could prime, load, and fire a musket three times in a minute. Soldiers had to be stationed close together (*close-order*) to concentrate the firepower of these weapons, which were inaccurate outside of 80 yards (72 meters). This meant that artillerymen were relatively safe from enemy musket fire, and bayonet charges were still possible. If the infantry ran as fast as they could, they could cover the last 80 yards during the twenty seconds that it took for defending infantrymen to reload their muskets.

Although wars were frequent in North America, large-scale battles were rare. American colonists lacked traditional military skills and organization and therefore learned from Native Americans to take their rifles and hide behind rocks and trees. This practical tactic, viewed as cowardly by some Europeans, effectively destroyed the old formation of exposed battle-line firing by platoons.

European armies were slow to adopt these new tactics in America. In 1755, in the French and Indian War, General Edward Braddock's force of British regulars was annihilated in western Pennsylvania by French and Native Americans firing under cover. Twenty years later, at the Battle of Bunker Hill in the American Revolution, the British were mauled as they attempted to storm American positions. In the War of 1812, the British formally attacked Andrew Jackson's well-defended positions in the Battle of New Orleans in 1815; it was less a battle than a slaughter. The British suffered more than 2,000 casualties with 300 killed. Only 13 Americans were killed, and fewer than 100 wounded or missing.

Nonetheless, the American army also relied on musket-armed line infantry in the early 1800s. Units with rifles were rare and usually served in support roles. Army officers understood the rifle's advantages, but they also were well aware that, as an 1819 ordnance report specifically stated, "the difficulty of loading this arm [is] the great objection to its more general introduction." Another official report noted that a soldier would have to stand up and expose himself to enemy fire in order to load a rifle because "the force necessary to drive a pitched ball down the rifle barrel, cannot be advantageously applied in any constrained position."

Warfare in North America differed from that traditionally practiced in Europe. Several North American battles of the eighteenth and early nineteenth centuries underscored the difference between traditional battle formations and firing from behind trees and rocks. This scene is from the battle at Lexington, Massachusetts, at the start of the Revolutionary War in April 1775.

In one 1828 test, thirty-seven soldiers firing muskets matched their skill for eight minutes against thirty-seven soldiers shooting Harpers Ferry Armory rifles. When the smoke cleared, the muskets had fired a total of 626 shots to the rifles' 420. A second test confirmed the result 845 to 494.

The Percussion Cap

The first of the major technological breakthroughs in firearms manufacture concerned not rifling the barrel or breech-loading, but the ignition system. Flintlocks operated on a simple idea: Sparks result when a sharp piece of flint—a type of stone—strikes steel. On a gun, these sparks could be made to fall into a small pan of gunpowder. The powder burned and transmitted the spark through the touchhole in the gun barrel into the main powder charge that fired the weapon. The system was not particularly reliable in the rain, especially because cartridges were held together with paper.

In 1807, Scottish minister Alexander Forsyth patented a percussion powder that could be used for priming a firearm; seven years later, Thomas Shaw of Philadelphia invented the percussion cap. The *percussion cap* was a small metal capsule filled with fulminate of mercury. When struck by the falling hammer of a gun lock, the capsule exploded and fired the gun instantly. This new ignition system dramatically reduced the number of misfires, especially in wet weather, and made any gun, from a long-barreled rifle to a handgun, more reliable.

By the 1840s, the old flintlock was obsolete. In 1844, the Springfield Armory started manufacturing percussion muskets, followed by Harpers Ferry the next year. By 1846, these two factories had built more than 17,000 new percussion muskets. During the Mexican War, they turned out another 78,000. The U.S. Army, however, was slow to adopt this technology. The War Department did not want soldiers to fight in Mexico with unfamiliar weapons and did not believe that there was enough time to train new volunteers. It also worried that soldiers would run out of percussion caps; in an emergency, a soldier could find a piece of flint lying on the ground, but only factories could turn out percussion caps.

However, some percussion cap rifles, known as Mississippi rifles, were used in the Mexican War. This weapon gained its name not because it came from Mississippi, but as a result of its performance in the hands of Jefferson Davis's Mississippi Regiment. Before setting out for Mexico, Davis had daringly requested 1,000 percussion rifles, even though the gun had not yet been introduced into the army. Over the objections of General Winfield Scott, Davis managed to have his entire regiment armed with the virtually untried gun. The percussion cap rifle performed well enough that even though it was obsolete by 1855, it was refitted to take the new bullets that had revolutionized rifle construction.

Changes in Bullets

In 1848, French army captain Claude Minié developed a bullet small enough to be rammed down a rifled barrel. The bullet had a wooden plug in its base that would expand on firing to engage the rifling. James Burton, a mechanic working at the Harpers Ferry Armory, developed an even better version. Burton's "cylindro-conoidal" bullet differed greatly from the typical round projectiles of the time. Burton's new bullets had a large cavity in the base that filled with gas and expanded the soft-metal rim when fired. This forced the bullet into the grooves of the rifling, even cleaning them as the bullet sped through the barrel.

Before the Civil War, the U.S. Army tended to leave the field-testing of new weapons to European nations at war. In the case of bullets, the War Department did not have long to wait. Expanding bullets such as "minié balls" and "Burton bullets" were proven effective in the Crimean War. Chief of Ordnance Colonel H. Craig reported in 1854, "The results stated to have been obtained in foreign service, and those derived from our own limited experiments, indicate so great a superiority of the rifled bore with the elongated expanding ball, that it seems probable that the use of smooth-bored arms and spherical balls may be entirely superseded."

The development of metal cartridges was the next step. A cartridge contains a charge of gunpowder with the bullet or shot wrapped in a casing of paper or metal. Samuel Pauly had invented the first cartridge containing its own primer in Switzerland in 1812. Many improvements in metallic cartridges were made in Europe in the 1830s and 1840s, but Americans excelled in manufacturing them. Between mid-1854 and mid-1855, the Allegheny Arsenal in Pittsburgh alone loaded 450,000 "rifle expanding bullet cartridges" and made more than 930,000 "rifle expanding bullets." By 1855, the smoothbore musket was effectively obsolete.

The Rifle-Musket

The combination of the Burton bullet, the percussion cap, and the rifled bore produced an accurate long-range weapon that required no ramming and was relatively

easy to load. In 1855, Congress, acting on the repeated
demands of President Franklin Pierce and Secretary of
War Jefferson Davis, increased the size of the regular
U.S. Army. As part of the military reorganization and
expansion, Davis switched the American army to the
.58-caliber rifle-musket, specifically designed to take the
new ammunition. When the first guns finally rolled out
of the armories in 1857, they still looked like muskets
with long barrels—usually 40 inches (101 centimeters).
However, they used minié balls, had rifled barrels, and
were fired by percussion caps. The Springfield Model
1855 was beautifully made, reliable, and accurate at long
range; ironically, it would be obsolete in ten years, but
not before it killed a few hundred thousand people in
the Civil War.

*The Springfield Model
1855 rifle-muskets used
in the Civil War were well
made and reliable,
although they would be
obsolete within ten years
of their manufacture.
This Civil War scene shows
Union troops assaulting
Fort Wagner, South
Carolina, in July 1863.*

FAST FACT

Secretary of War Jefferson Davis would later regret the day that he switched the U.S. Army to rifle-muskets. As president of the Confederacy, Davis had the rueful satisfaction of knowing the effectiveness of those guns against his own forces.

Because the Model 1855 loaded at the muzzle, it was still slow and awkward to load. In order to use the rifle-musket, a soldier had to rip open a paper-wrapped cartridge of gunpowder with his teeth, pour the powder and bullet down the barrel, jam them in tight with a ramrod, cock the hammer halfway to insert a percussion cap, and then finally cock the hammer again. Only then was he ready to aim and fire the gun. No wonder the most competent soldiers could still fire no more than three shots a minute. A few skillful soldiers could do all this while lying on their backs, but most had to load from a kneeling or standing position—a definite disadvantage when facing enemies who were trying to kill them. Nonetheless, the accuracy of the rifle-musket made it a vast improvement over previous long arms.

Samuel Colt and the Revolver

While long guns were changing so dramatically, handguns were not left behind. The first known revolvers were invented in the late 1500s, and the "pepperbox," a multifiring gun like a pistol, appeared in the early 1800s. Three Americans—Elisha Collier, Cornelius Coolidge, and Artemas Wheeler—invented and promoted a flintlock revolver in 1818. The flintlock mechanism, however, was less than ideal for rapid, repeating fire. Although the concept of a revolver had existed for centuries, it was never a military or commercial success until the percussion cap replaced the flintlock in the early 1800s.

Samuel Colt patented his breech-loading revolving pistol in England and France in 1835 and the United States in 1836. There did not appear to be any market for the weapon, and Colt's New Jersey–based Patent Fire-Arms Manufacturing Company closed in 1842. For the next five years, Colt concentrated on submarine explosive devices, but he returned to firearms when General Zachary Taylor, the commander of United States forces in the Mexican War, requested that the War Department purchase Colt's handguns. Colt turned his first profit in 1849; by 1854, he was building the largest private armory in the world in Hartford, Connecticut.

Colt's original revolver was single-action, which meant that the hammer had to be cocked by the thumb to revolve the cylinder. However, Colt created the market, and his invention triggered a flood of improvements from competitors such as the Joslyn Arms Company and Savage and North in Connecticut and the Remington Arms Company and the Starr Arms Company in New York. By 1860, so-called double-action made it possible to fire the revolver even more quickly, and it would become a favorite gun of Western settlers.

At the famous Crystal Palace Exposition in London in 1851, the U.S. exhibit drew praise for the quality of its manufactured goods. Colt's revolvers especially won rave reviews, and both military men and civilians placed orders. On July 5, 1851, the *Illustrated London News* carried a diagram of Colt's revolver, stating that it was "so terribly efficient in its operation as to leave all former inventions of the kind far in the background." Colt's weapon became so popular that the term *Colt* was sometimes used as a synonym for *revolver*.

Beecher's Bibles

In September 1848, former Harpers Ferry employee Christian Sharps patented a breech-loading design that would become famous all over the western United States. Despite mechanical problems, the gun could sometimes fire as many as ten shots a minute. Until the late 1850s, it was the only breech-loading rifle that was a commercial success.

The Sharps rifle acquired national fame after the passage of the Kansas-Nebraska Act in 1854. The act resulted in a bloody guerrilla war in Kansas between pro- and antislavery forces over whether Kansas would be a free state or a slave state. Prominent New Englanders aided Kansas abolitionists in "Bleeding Kansas" by raising money for them to purchase Sharps rifles. The first shipment of rifles arrived in Lawrence, Kansas, in crates supposedly containing books. Sharps rifles became known as "Beecher's Bibles" after Henry Ward Beecher, the famous Brooklyn, New York, abolitionist, who said, "You might as well...read the Bible to buffaloes as to [supporters of slavery]; but they have a supreme respect for the logic that is embodied in a Sharps rifle."

Nonetheless, the U.S. Army still hesitated to adopt breech-loading rifles. Major Alfred Mordecai, the government's leading ordnance expert, admitted in 1856, "Loading at the breech, if it can be accomplished in a perfect manner, offers a complete solution of the question of easy loading and close fitting." Unfortunately, he added, "mechanical ingenuity seems to have been thus far incapable of removing all the difficulties of having an opening or joint exposed to the action of a charge of powder." In addition, army officers feared (rightly, as it turned out) that faster firing rifles would lead soldiers to waste ammunition by firing more often.

The End of the Harpers Ferry Arsenal

In October 1859, the Harpers Ferry arsenal became the subject of national headlines when John Brown, a fervent abolitionist, and twenty-one followers captured it with almost no resistance. Brown apparently hoped to distribute the weapons to escaped slaves and flee to the nearby Blue Ridge Mountains, where he could stir up further slave rebellions. He was slow to leave Harpers Ferry, however, and was captured in a shootout with U.S. Marines in which ten of Brown's men died. He was tried and hanged in nearby Charles Town in December—a freedom fighter and martyr to some, and a terrorist and murderer to others.

At the time of Abraham Lincoln's election in 1860, the United States possessed twenty-eight arsenals, armories, and weapons depots scattered across the country and operated by the Ordnance Department. Eleven of these were seized by the Confederacy as soon as the Civil War began, but the most important prize was the federal arsenal at Harpers Ferry. A week after the Confederate attack on Fort Sumter in 1861, the Virginia militia moved on Harpers

Ferry; the small Union garrison, seeing that there was no way to defend the place, intentionally burned the arsenal, including 15,000 long guns. Virginians carted away some of the salvaged machinery, but the illustrious sixty-year history of the Harpers Ferry arsenal had come to an end.

Between April 1861 and the end of the Civil War four years later, the strategic town of Harpers Ferry would change hands at least eleven times. The Baltimore and Ohio (B&O) railroad bridge that crossed the Potomac River at the town was destroyed and rebuilt nine times. The town's industrial buildings were almost completely destroyed; ironically, one of the only buildings to remain standing was the little engine house where John Brown had made his final stand in 1859; it still remains to this day.

This is what the Harpers Ferry arsenal looked like in 1862, a year after it ceased operations as a federal arsenal. The fact that it was a sought-after prize in the Civil War led to its demise. The engine house where John Brown made his last stand can be seen at left, just inside the gate.

The Rifle-Musket and the Civil War

When the Civil War began, the Union held approximately 600,000 guns in storage, but only about 8 percent had rifled bores. The Confederates' destruction of the arsenal at Harpers Ferry complicated the supply problem. Although production at Springfield increased from 800 to 6,900 rifles a month between April and October 1861, the U.S. government was forced to contract with private manufacturers and even import firearms from Europe. Despite the inevitable delays, Northern factories eventually produced more than 2 million rifle-muskets during the five-year war; by 1865, Springfield alone could produce more than 275,000 rifles a year.

The American Civil War was one of the first wars fought with new industrial technology such as railroad transport, ironclad ships, and highly efficient and increasingly deadly firearms. In the Mexican War, the U.S. Army had generally used single-shot, smoothbore, muzzle-loading muskets. With this type of weapon, a good marksman could hit a target at 80 yards (72 meters), but anything beyond 100 yards (90 meters) was pretty safe. A soldier of average height who fired his musket with the barrel parallel to the ground could expect his bullet to hit the earth only about 120 yards (108 meters) away from where he stood; anything 250 yards (225 meters) distant was simply out of reach. Union general (and later U.S. president) Ulysses Grant observed in his memoirs, "At a distance of a few hundred yards a man might fire at you all day without your finding out about it."

By 1863, almost all infantrymen on both sides carried rifles; Union infantrymen used Springfield rifle-muskets while Confederates carried Enfields, similar weapons made in Great Britain. The change to rifle-muskets altered military tactics beyond recognition. The rifle-musket was sturdy, relatively reliable in bad weather, simple to operate, fairly cheap to manufacture, and most importantly, had an effective killing range of 300 yards (270 meters)—or even 400 yards (360 meters). Although it was slow and cumbersome, the rifle-musket's extended range revolutionized the battlefield. Close-order battle formations and charges became almost useless, as soldiers

> **FAST FACT**
>
> Although the trench warfare around Petersburg, Virginia, in 1864 provided an ominous preview of the shape of future wars, European military observers tended to ignore the evidence before their eyes. Trench warfare and the invention of the machine gun would make World War I (1914–1918) even more of a bloodbath.

with rifles cut down the waves of attacking infantrymen; bayonets accounted for less than 1 percent of all wounds in the Civil War. Cavalry riders were virtually driven from the battlefield when faced with rifles accurate over almost 400 yards; they dismounted and fired their own long-range weapons. Even artillery was initially a less effective defense against the new weapons, because sharpshooters could now pick off artillerymen and enemy officers. The infantry and artillery tactics of Napoleon's day, taught so diligently at West Point, had become obsolete.

By 1863, it became apparent to most open-minded observers that an infantry armed with rifle-muskets and firing from a protected position could turn back forces three to four times its size. Some officers began to have their soldiers dig trenches, throw up breastworks, and emphasize the defensive over the offensive. However, generals on both sides were slow to understand the meaning of the new technology. In numerous battles (Fredericksburg, Gettysburg, and Cold Harbor are the best examples), generals ordered thousands of infantrymen into dense close-order formation and sent them against

The use of the rifle-musket in the Civil War changed battle tactics that had been used for centuries. Many military commanders recognized the weapon's potential, but they were often slow to change their tactics. The result was higher casualties. In this engraving, Confederates charge up a hill known as Little Round Top during the Battle of Gettysburg in Pennsylvania in 1863.

Muskets were not the only weapons to use rifle technology. Blakely rifle cannons, pictured here in Charleston, South Carolina, in 1863, were used extensively during the Civil War, mostly by the Confederate Army.

enemy positions in successive waves. In most cases, the charging infantrymen were mowed down.

Confederate general Robert E. Lee continued to use daring and aggressive offensive tactics that resulted in thousands of casualties that the Confederacy could ill afford to lose, because the North had more soldiers than the South. Then when Confederate general Joseph Johnston successfully used strategic retreat and delay to fight Union general William T. Sherman in the Atlanta campaign, Jefferson Davis, president of the Confederacy, fired him for lack of fighting spirit. His replacement, John Bell Hood, said, "We should attack," promptly lost 15,000 men (to Sherman's 6,000) in eight days, and then managed to have his army annihilated at the Battle of Nashville. The Confederate military tactic of "attack and die" played a major role in the Confederacy's failure to win the Civil War.

The Slow Development of Breechloaders

Almost as soon as firearms were invented, soldiers and gunsmiths realized that loading at the breech would be safer and much faster than loading at the muzzle. For centuries, however, the technology did not exist to make breech-loading truly practical. Just the same, several American inventors had developed breech-loading weapons by 1861. The most famous breechloader was John Hall's Model 1819, first produced at Harpers Ferry in 1824 using a patent that Hall had received in 1811. However, these early models were considered too complicated for soldiers who were often barely literate; the ordnance board that reviewed Hall's breechloader in 1836 commented that "an arm which is complicated in its mechanism and arrangement deranges and perplexes the soldier."

In the 1840s, cartridges containing the primer, bullet, and powder were wrapped in paper. This meant that gas, and sometimes even fire, escaped from the breech, occasionally making the weapon as dangerous to the shooter as to its intended victim. When the Ordnance Department adopted a new rifle in 1841, it again chose a muzzleloader over a breechloader, despite the thousands of dollars spent on Hall's manufacture and trials. During the Civil War, the Union manufactured or purchased 2.85 million muzzle-loading rifles, 303,000 breech-loading repeating rifles, and 100,000 single-shot breech-loading rifles. Yet although Union cavalry and some infantry units carried breechloaders (mostly Sharps rifles) by the end of the Civil War, they remained unreliable. Breechloaders, known as "needle guns" in Europe, were not widely accepted there either.

The Breech-Loading Revolution

In an amazingly short period around mid-century, breechloaders became standard issue. The key development was the replacement of paper cartridges by increasingly advanced metallic cartridges in the 1840s. This not only prevented the escape of gas at the breech, but also made the gun safer, more durable, and more reliable in wet weather. The spread of metallic cartridges completely did away with awkward loading and powder-carrying equipment. Unlike paper cartridges, however, metallic cartridges could be made only by workers in factories, not by soldiers in regiments.

Between 1860 and 1871, almost 500 patents were taken out on breech-loading mechanisms in the United States, and the concept was essentially perfected. The speed of firing was increased by the *bolt action,* a breech bolt that inserted the ball and cartridge, sealed the breech, locked the cartridge or shell into firing position, and cocked the firing pin. An extractor on the bolt removed the empty case from the chamber. *Single-shot action* removed the fired cartridge and replaced it with a fresh cartridge in one movement. The gradual replacement of iron by steel increased the life of the gun barrel and reduced the number of explosions due to barrel defects.

Breechloaders gave yet another huge advantage to the defense on the battlefield. In 1866, Prussians (Germans) using breechloaders outfired Austrians with muzzleloaders by a ratio of six to one in the Seven Weeks War. Direct attacks against infantry became almost suicidal, and maneuver and flank attacks became more important. One officer stated that "within effective range, breech-loading rifles are infinitely more destructive than artillery.... Now artillerymen even at 1,000 yards [900 meters] are exposed to an accurate and rapid fire from the enemy's infantry."

The Spencer and the Rise of Repeating Rifles

The rapid improvements in metallic cartridges also allowed firearms inventors to experiment with box- or tubular-shaped devices for storing cartridges in the rifle itself. If this type of "magazine rifle" were possible, then maybe a feeding mechanism could be invented that would send the live cartridges into the chamber automatically. In 1860, Christopher Spencer, a former Colt machinist, patented a breech-loading rifle that contained a magazine of seven spring-fed metallic cartridges in a tube. A lever-action trigger guard fed and ejected cartridges and empty cases at breathtaking speed. The Spencer rifle could fire seven bullets in twelve seconds or twenty-one in a minute. Major General James Wilson tested the Spencer and called it "the best fire-arm yet put in the hands of the soldier...I have never seen anything else like the confidence inspired by it."

In December 1864, General Alexander Dyer, chief of the Ordnance Department, wrote to Secretary of War Edwin Stanton that the "experience of the war has shown that breech-loading arms are greatly superior to muzzle loaders for infantry as well as for cavalry, and that measures should immediately be taken to substitute a suitable breech-loading musket in place of the rifle musket." He recommended that a board of army officers meet at the Springfield Armory to "examine, test and

This Union cavalry officer was photographed with his saber and his Spencer carbine at his side. The word "carbine" denotes a gun with a short barrel. Cavalry riders favored these guns because they were easy to handle on horseback.

recommend for adoption a suitable breechloader for muskets and carbines, and a suitable repeater or magazine carbine, and that the arm recommended by the board may, if approved by the War Department, be exclusively adopted for the military service." In 1865, the trial board established by General Dyer tested sixty-five different repeating breech-loading rifles using metallic cartridges; the board chose the Spencer repeating rifle as the best model. Nonetheless, the Spencer Firearms Company went bankrupt in 1869, a victim of the astounding surplus of firearms after the Civil War.

Springfield and the Allin Conversion

After the Civil War ended, the Union almost completely demobilized its army. In April 1865, the U.S. Army boasted more than 1 million men in uniform, with an annual budget of $31 million. One year later, the army had a strength of less than 60,000 men and a budget of only $700,000. Tens of thousands of obsolete muzzleloaders were stacked as war surplus in armories. As the federal budget tightened, the plans to adopt the Spencer rifle or any other multishot breechloader were abandoned. Converting the army to a repeating rifle would require the purchase of entirely new and expensive machinery. Instead, Congress and the Ordnance Department tried to save money by turning the existing stores of muzzle-loading rifles that jammed the armories into single-shot breechloaders.

Working at Springfield in 1865, master armorer Erskine Allin devised the "Allin Conversion." This simple process enabled the War Department to change outdated muzzleloaders into breechloaders at a very small cost, thus avoiding the complete replacement of the military's supply of weapons. The Allin Conversion was performed by opening the breech section of the musket barrel and inserting a *breech block* (a metal block designed to accept a metallic cartridge). The breech block was hinged to the barrel to allow it to tilt up for loading cartridges. After firing, an ejector on the breech block removed the used cartridge.

The Springfield Armory had emerged from the Civil War as the main site for American firearms research and development. Between 1866 and 1881, the facilities were expanded with the addition of a ballistic research laboratory and an experimental firing house. During the Civil War, the armory had manufactured tens of thousands of Springfield Model 1863 rifle-muskets needed to preserve the Union. However, after the war, the armory failed to produce newer and more efficient weapons, like those manufactured by the civilian firearms suppliers. While companies like Winchester were turning out thousands of repeating rifles, the Ordnance Department, subject to a decreasing budget, was trying to fight Native Americans in the West with the Springfield Model 1873 "trapdoor" rifle. This rifle was actually little more than a modified 1855 Springfield rifle with the Allin Conversion.

Competition in Handguns

By Samuel Colt's death in 1862, his revolver was only one of many handguns on the market. Two noted companies— Smith & Wesson and Derringer—became famous for producing lethal weapons that could be easily concealed.

This competition in handguns was also aided by the development of metallic cartridges. In 1856, Horace Smith and Daniel Wesson produced the first practical self-contained metallic cartridge and the revolver that fired it. Smith and Wesson had first formed their partnership in 1852 in Springfield. Although the army didn't adopt a revolver using metallic cartridges before the Civil War, army and navy officers bought thousands of them with their own money. In 1859, the demand for handguns was so great that the Smith & Wesson company had to build a new factory in Springfield, close to the U.S. Armory. By 1865, so many people wanted its .22-caliber and .32-caliber revolvers that Smith & Wesson had orders for two years in advance. The company hurtled past Colt, whose revolver models still used paper cartridges and separate percussion caps. In 1869, Smith & Wesson sold $180,000 worth of revolvers, one-third more than Colt. For the next century, Smith & Wesson would be a world leader in handgun design and technology.

In 1852, Henry Deringer (with one *r*) had patented his first handgun. The original Deringer was a very small, single-barrel, .41-caliber percussion pistol that could be easily hidden in a shooter's hand. The Deringer was specifically designed to be concealed; John Wilkes Booth used one to assassinate President Abraham Lincoln in 1865. Competing gun manufacturers, trying to capitalize on the popularity of these small weapons, called their pistols "derringers" (with two *r*'s). Derringers were not repeaters; in order to fire without reloading, extra gun barrels were required. The most famous type of derringer was the Remington over/under (two-barrel) design that was copied by many other companies and is still used today. Derringers were only useful for very close-range personal protection. According to legend, they were the favorite weapons of card sharks of the old West, perhaps because their short barrels and lack of sights made them ineffective at almost any range beyond the length of a card table. Derringers also achieved great popularity as weapons of self-defense in American cities in the 1880s and 1890s.

This is the handgun that John Wilkes Booth used to assassinate President Abraham Lincoln in 1865.

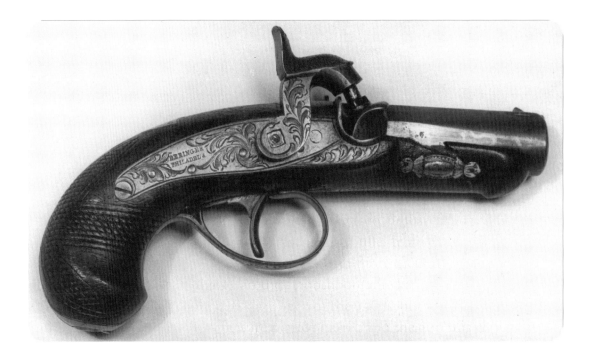

Remington and Winchester

Eliphalet Remington, a blacksmith who switched to gunsmithing, began producing handmade rifles in 1816. He eventually founded a company on the Erie Canal in Ilion, New York, that supplied the U.S. Army with rifles in the Mexican War. His son, Philo Remington, ran the firm during the Civil War, when it was one of the most important private manufacturers of guns for the Union army. After the war, the state-of-the-art Remington Rolling Block rifle (first produced in 1865) became popular in the western United States.

Oliver Winchester was a cagey investor who had made some money in sewing machines. He then invested in Smith & Wesson's first handgun factory and later owned a stake in the New Haven Arms Company. In 1860, Benjamin Tyler Henry, the chief designer for this firm, had used a breech-loading rifle invented by Walter B. Hunt to create a new lever-action repeating rifle. The New Haven Arms Company manufactured about 13,000 of these "Henry rifles." In 1866, Winchester took control of the company and changed the name to the Winchester Repeating Arms Company. The first Winchester, the Model 1866, used a totally round magazine tube, designed by foreman Nelson King, which avoided the problem of dirt getting into the works. A later version, the 1873 Winchester repeating rifle, was probably the most popular long gun in the western United States.

> **FAST FACT**
>
> Remington's company would later diversify into manufacturing a host of different products, including silverware, hunting knives, cash registers, and sewing machines. Its most famous effort was the Remington typewriter, first produced in 1873.

Final Developments of the Century

The increased rate of fire of repeating breechloaders led to problems. The black powder in use at the time hindered the rifleman's vision and immediately revealed the shooter's position. In 1886, French chemist Paul Vielle succeeded in perfecting a smokeless powder that burned more completely and would not corrode guns. The new powder again changed military tactics, allowing an individual rifleman or machine-gun team time to aim and fire from a camouflaged position. A Swiss officer then produced a copper-jacketed, lead-cored bullet suited to the high speeds produced by the smokeless powder. This bullet had increased range and greater penetrating power.

By 1890, the firearms industry had developed magazine loading, smokeless powder, and bolt action. Weapons using these improvements were used by armies around the world. These innovations marked the end of a series of advances in firearms ammunition that began around 1800. The century had brought enormous changes to the firearms industry. The muzzle-loading flintlock, which had been the mainstay of both armies and civilians in 1800, now seemed as obsolete as the crossbow. In the twentieth century, the firearms industry would work on creating even deadlier handheld automatic weapons.

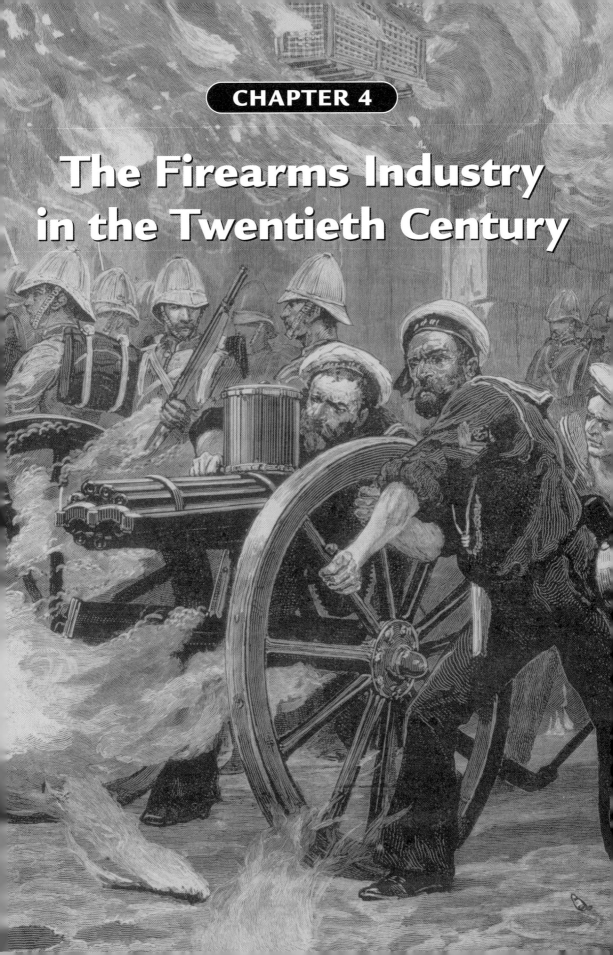

CHAPTER 4

The Firearms Industry in the Twentieth Century

Firearms became ever more powerful in the twentieth century. In 1900, American soldiers still used repeating rifles with bayonets. The deployment of the machine gun in the early 1900s, the semiautomatic M-1 after World War I (1914–1918), and the fully automatic M-16 after World War II (1939–1945) meant that light, handheld weapons could now spray a blizzard of bullets across any battlefield. Yet strangely enough, firearms declined in importance, even as the United States adopted a large standing army in the second half of the century. The development of extremely lethal and expensive weapons such as armored tanks, jet airplanes, submarines with missiles, and nuclear weapons reduced the importance of the infantryman with his handheld weapon. The U.S. Army has seen no reason to replace the M-16 since its introduction in the 1960s; the days of the firearms industry spearheading a technological revolution are gone.

On the civilian front, American gun manufacturers have had to balance competing interests. Although their sales increased dramatically after 1960, they also had to face a good deal of public condemnation. Increasing crime, large-scale race riots, and notorious political assassinations all combined to make the issue of gun control central to politics in the United States. Americans began to argue whether there were too many guns in civilian hands. The firearms industry would be forced to respond.

Salvation in Exports

Before 1865, despite Samuel Colt's dabbling in international markets, the United States imported far more weapons and gun parts than it exported. The situation changed drastically after the Civil War. Like many other American industries, firearms companies now produced more than Americans could possibly buy. Yet total U.S. Army expenditures had shrunk from $284 million in 1866 to $32 million in 1878; they were still only $55 million in 1894, only four years before the Spanish-American War (1898). If American firearm manufacturers hoped to stay in business, they would have to find new markets for their products. They did this by supplying foreign nations with guns.

American manufacturers rearmed all major European armies with rifled breechloaders in the late 1860s and 1870s. Between 1868 and 1878, the United States exported an average of $4.1 million worth of firearms every year. Remington pioneered the foreign gun trade in breechloaders, while Smith & Wesson began heavily pushing revolvers overseas. Both companies saved themselves from bankruptcy by discovering the export trade. In 1871, the Russian government ordered 20,000 Model 3 revolvers from Smith & Wesson. The contract influenced the worldwide market, and the company, formerly on the brink of bankruptcy, ran its factories at full capacity and gained international prestige.

Europeans noticed the new reach and strength of the American firearms industry. The London *Daily Telegraph* complained in 1877 about "the execution of such large orders [of firearms] by America—few seem to have come to England, our export of arms and ammunition having fallen off instead of increasing lately.... [The Americans] accept orders for such goods as firearms on a scale which our

Philo Remington, pictured here about 1870, took over the firearms factory his father had started in time to take advantage of new opportunities in the export of guns to foreign countries. Both Remington and Smith & Wesson saved their companies from bankruptcy this way after sales fell off after the Civil War.

makers obviously cannot undertake." In 1881, a Russian observed, "Just as European factories had earlier supplied America with arms, so America, in turn, is now the great industrial power. Its products are capable of glutting all the European arms markets and with little strain filling the enormous orders of European governments."

Americans also excelled at producing the new metallic cartridges so highly desired by European armies. In 1882, a firearms specialist bragged, "The best evidence of the high value placed upon cartridges manufactured by Union Metallic Cartridge Company [owned by Remington] is the fact that the governments of Russia, Germany, France, and Spain have established manufactories for making the system of cartridges which has been adopted by them as ammunition in their respective countries." Exporting guns and cartridges overseas kept American firearms factories busy in the early twentieth century when the demand for guns was met at home. As a result, American advances in firearms and in manufacturing methods spread around the world.

Buy American?

Even as American firearms exports increased, the U.S. Army was relying more heavily on foreign advances in gun design. In 1890, an American military board began an eighteen-month study to decide on a replacement for the Springfield single-shot rifles being used by American armed forces. After comparing about forty different rifle designs, they adopted the Krag-Jorgenson rifle designed by two Norwegian armorers.

Many Americans were upset that the United States, a leader in firearms manufacturing, should use a European design for the national rifle. The Fortifications Appropriations Act of 1888, while saying nothing about design, had required that "all guns and materials purchased under the authority of this section shall be of American production and furnished by citizens of the United States." American rifle manufacturers pressured

the U.S. government into conducting a second round of tests in April and May of 1893. Still, none of the other rifles met the War Department's requirements and the Krag was put into production in 1894.

The Springfield Armory eventually produced more than 440,000 Krag rifles and 60,000 Krag carbines, with a one-dollar royalty for each U.S. Magazine Rifle, Model 1892, paid to the two Norwegian inventors. Although the Krag was sometimes considered slow to reload, a skilled shooter could now fire twenty shots in a minute. American forces in the Spanish-American War, the Philippine-American War (1899–1901), and the Boxer Rebellion (1900) all used the Krag rifle.

French troops undergo inspection during the Boxer Rebellion in China in 1900. The goal of this uprising by a Chinese secret society was to expel all foreigners from the country. It was put down by forces from many countries, including the United States, whose soldiers were armed with Norwegian-designed Krag rifles.

Old Reliable

During the Spanish-American War, American soldiers felt that the (German) Mauser rifle used by Spanish soldiers loaded faster than the "trapdoor" Springfield or the Krag service rifle used by the U.S. Army. In addition, weaknesses in the bolt of the American rifle reduced its accuracy and prevented it from using high-speed ammunition. In 1900, the U.S. Army began working on a

FAST FACT

The Springfield Armory built a special Model 1903, Serial #6000, for Theodore Roosevelt. The president killed more than 300 animals with this rifle on his hunting trips.

new rifle; it was adopted as the .30-caliber U.S. Rifle Model 1903 on June 20, 1903.

By the time the United States entered World War I in 1917, more than 800,000 Model 1903 rifles had been manufactured at the arsenals in Rock Island, Illinois, and Springfield. Springfield produced another 265,000 of them during the war. When World War I ended, U.S. factories were churning out M1917s (modified versions of the M1903) at the rate of 10,000 per day. The M1903 turned out to be an exceedingly durable rifle. It served as the standard service long arm of the American army for a record thirty-three years, until it was replaced by the M-1 in 1937. The M-16 has since broken this record.

In this 1890 illustration, a naval officer operates a Gatling gun mounted on a ship. Although the Gatling gun, which represented the first attempt to manufacture a machine gun, was used by the military throughout the last decades of the nineteenth century, it was never widely used in battle.

The Gatling Gun

From the first appearance of firearms, inventors had tinkered with the idea of creating a weapon that spewed out vast numbers of bullets with one press of the trigger. The first attempts to multiply firepower in this way appeared as early as the 1300s. Until the nineteenth

century, however, it was simply beyond anyone's technological ability to create this type of weapon in an age of flintlocks and muzzleloaders.

In December 1862, Richard Gatling, a Southern-born doctor, demonstrated for the Union army a primitive machine gun that could fire 200 rounds per minute. Gatling's gun was the best of several rapid-fire types tested by the United States during the Civil War. The manual, crank-operated gun used six to ten barrels set around an axis. By turning the crank, the gun could be made to fire repeatedly using the force of the gun's recoil and expanding gases. The multiple barrels and the heavy construction made the Gatling gun too large to be carried by hand. Instead, it was mounted on a carriage, like a light artillery piece. In August 1866, too late to be useful in the Civil War, the Ordnance Department contracted for 100 of these guns, to be produced at the Colt Armory in Hartford at a cost of $162,000.

The Gatling gun did not receive much actual usage by the U.S. Army. Between 1874 and 1878, it was used only six times against Native Americans. A heavy machine gun had limited value in this kind of warfare, which required very mobile cavalry, not slow-moving artillery units. However, soldiers did get to fire the Gatling gun in the massacre of the Sioux at Wounded Knee in 1890. State governments and private companies also dragged out the Gatling gun during the frequent strikes and labor disputes that convulsed the late 1800s; though it was rarely fired, it served quite well to intimidate workers.

Improvements in the Machine Gun

When Hiram Maxim, a Maine-born American engineer, moved to Great Britain, a friend told him, "If you want to make your fortune, invent something which will allow those fool Europeans to kill each other more quickly." In 1884, Maxim patented a more advanced model of Gatling's gun. Until Maxim's invention, weapons of this type required the muscle power of the operator to fire,

Hiram Maxim's trigger-fired machine gun, patented in 1884, the year after this photograph of the inventor and his gun was taken, required less effort to operate and could fire more rounds per minute than the Gatling gun. Even so, Maxim's gun was never adopted by the U.S. military, mainly for political reasons.

usually by turning a crank. The Maxim did not require a crank, but fired when the trigger was depressed and continued firing until it was released or the gun ran out of cartridges. By using the weapon's recoil to reload, the water-cooled Maxim gun could fire 600 rounds a minute. Because self-acting or automatic mechanisms in industry were called "machines," Maxim's automatic gun became known as a "machine gun." Yet despite Maxim's invention, the Gatling gun remained the standard U.S. Army machine gun until 1903. The Gatling gun was made in Connecticut, the home state of Senator Joseph Hawley, chair of the Senate Committee on Military Affairs; the Maxim gun was manufactured in Britain.

Because the machine guns of the time looked like artillery pieces, the U.S. Army tended to think of them as inferior cannons. As late as 1911, U.S. Army drill regulations listed the machine gun under the heading "miscellaneous" and called it a "weapon of emergency" that was valuable only at "infrequent" periods. American military theory of the time clearly stated, "Firepower alone cannot be depended upon to stop an attack." Nonetheless, machine guns were widely used by European imperialist powers against native peoples in Africa and Asia; the United States also deployed them against the anti-imperialist Boxers in China in 1900 and against the Philippine independence movement.

Around the time of World War I, American-born inventors working in Europe, such as Isaac Lewis and John Browning, pioneered further improvements in the machine gun. By the time the United States entered the war in 1917, the U.S. Army had developed a relatively lightweight, tripod-mounted machine gun that could be transported by pack animals, but army officials were not sure what to do with this weapon. In 1917, the United States possessed fewer than 2,000 machine guns and had none on order. In contrast, the Germans had gone to war three years earlier with 12,000 late-model Maxims and 50,000 on order. The U.S. Army would learn the importance of the machine gun the hard way, but by late 1918, factories were producing machine guns at the rate of 27,000 a month.

> **FAST FACT**
>
> Hiram Maxim became a British citizen and was knighted in 1900. His brother and son remained in the United States. They were renowned inventors of explosives, smokeless powder, and a "silencer" for weapons.

The Machine Gun and World War I

The machine gun completed the firearms revolution that had begun before the American Civil War. It changed the nature of combat by completely mechanizing killing. The things that had defined warfare for thousands of years— courage, individual heroism, the glorious charge—all went down, swept away by a deadly hail of bullets. What the rifle had done to the bayonet in the Civil War, the machine gun did to the rifle in World War I.

Machine guns, used as infantry weapons instead of as part of the artillery, worked with deadly efficiency. By sweeping the area between the two sides' trenches—known as "no-man's-land"—with a firestorm of lead, the machine gun almost completely prevented any offensive tactics. Neither masses of horse cavalry nor even loose-order infantry could conquer a position defended by machine-gun fire, barbed wire, and trenches. All the advantages rested with the defensive. In the next war, the tank and the airplane would end the machine gun's domination. In World War I, however, these two counterweapons were not particularly advanced, nor did conservative army staffs understand their revolutionary potential. Instead, the clattering sound of machine guns spraying no-man's-land would haunt European and American consciousness for a generation.

By the end of World War I in 1918, the Allies (the United States, Great Britain, France, and Russia) and Central Powers (Germany, Austria-Hungary, and the Ottoman Empire) had managed to kill more than 8 million of each other's soldiers. The United States had cleverly stayed out of the bloodbath until 1917, but even so, more than 40,000 Americans were killed in action in less than a year's fighting.

The Tommy Gun and the Roaring Twenties

When World War I ended, the American firearms industry began designing a submachine gun, a light weapon that could be fired from either the hip or shoulder but could be carried around by a single person. Most early machine guns could not be carried by an individual soldier because of their weight. Although the Germans and Italians used primitive submachine guns in World War I, the American firearms industry came up with the best model after the war.

In the United States, General John Thompson had developed a stellar record modernizing and producing firearms at the Springfield and Rock Island armories and working for the Ordnance Department in Washington, D.C. After World War I, Thompson formed Auto-Ordnance, a private firearms company. Working with John Blish, Theodore Eickhoff, and Oscar Payne, Thompson perfected the Thompson submachine gun in 1920. The handheld, self-oiling gun fired more than 500 .45-caliber cartridges a minute—almost 10 a second.

Thompson wanted the Colt Company to manufacture the submachine gun under contract; instead, Colt offered Auto-Ordnance $1 million for the rights. Thompson turned down the offer, saying, "If it's worth a million to them, it's worth a million to us." However, he had failed to consider that with the end of World War I and no new conflict on the horizon, his weapon had little peacetime sales potential.

Thompson's best market for submachine guns turned out to be the gangsters of the Prohibition era (the 1920s), who made the "tommy gun" famous throughout the world. In New York City, after the passage of gun control legislation known as the Sullivan Law in 1911, a person could not even buy a .22 target revolver without a license and without registering the gun. That person could, however, buy a Thompson submachine gun, because the law did not cover them. Criminals bought the weapon from neighborhood gun dealers who did not ask too many questions.

The tommy gun initially appeared in organized gang warfare in September 1925 but became nationally notorious with the first "machine gun massacre" in April 1926. In the "Siege of Cicero" in Illinois in September 1926, Hymie Weiss's men loaded into eleven cars and fired more than 1,000 bullets into Al Capone's headquarters; in return,

General John Thompson demonstrates his submachine gun in 1922. Unlike previous machine guns, it was light enough to be carried and fired by hand. Much to the general's dismay, that was one reason that the "tommy gun" became so popular with gangsters, who made up the only real market for such weapons in the 1920s.

Weiss was mowed down by machine gun fire twenty-one days later. In the climactic St. Valentine's Day Massacre of 1929, Capone's gang (headed by "Machine Gun" Jack McGurn) killed seven members of Chicago's North Side gang, shooting them in their backs with machine guns. In cities across the United States, the "chopper" became a standard weapon of criminal gangs, much to John Thompson's dismay. Along with jazz and speakeasies, the tommy gun became a symbol of the Roaring Twenties.

Machine Guns in the 1930s

In the early years of the Great Depression, movies featuring gangsters blazing away at each other from the hip with tommy guns were often box office smashes. *The Public Enemy*, starring James Cagney, and *Little Caesar*, featuring Edward G. Robinson, both appeared in 1930, followed by *Smart Money* in 1931 and *Scarface* in 1932. These films popularized the use of automatic weaponry; critics claimed that they glorified violence and lawlessness, but the moviegoing public adored them. In the midst of the economic downturn, many Americans also took a tolerant view of the bank robberies, kidnappings, and gun battles that flared across the Midwest. The escapades of George "Machine Gun" Kelly, John

Famous bandits Bonnie Parker and Clyde Barrow were apprehended by police near Arcadia, Louisiana, on May 24, 1934. Police fired 167 bullets into their car, shown here, killing them both. Bonnie and Clyde were part of the culture of tommy guns and bank robberies that so fascinated Americans in the 1930s.

Dillinger, Charles "Pretty Boy" Floyd, Kate "Ma" Barker, and Bonnie Parker and Clyde Barrow both entertained and horrified the nation.

By 1939, Auto-Ordnance had sold only 10,300 submachine guns in two decades—4,700 in the United States, 4,100 in foreign countries, and 1,500 to the U.S. government. The outbreak of World War II finally made the weapon profitable. Every Allied country, including the United States, demanded Thompson submachine guns; the plants in Utica, New York, and Bridgeport, Connecticut, eventually turned out almost 2 million of them. In the U.S. Army, Thompson's gun was used alongside the more advanced M-3, which was popularly known as the "grease gun" because of its resemblance to the device used to lubricate cars.

The Beginning of Regulation

On February 15, 1933, Giuseppe Zangara attempted to assassinate Franklin Roosevelt while the president-elect was speaking in Miami, Florida. Zangara, who bought his .32-caliber pistol for four dollars at a local drugstore, failed to harm Roosevelt but killed Anton Cermak, the mayor of Chicago. The assassination horrified many Americans, who already believed that violence had increased tremendously in the 1920s and 1930s. Reformers proposed that gun owners should be licensed and pistols should be banned completely. The firearms industry was not totally opposed to some restrictions. Street murders, even of criminals, were not good publicity for gun manufacturers.

As a compromise, Congress eventually passed the National Firearms Act of 1934 (and its weaker cousin, the Firearms Act of 1938). This legislation, the first national gun control laws, taxed the manufacture, sale, and transfer of certain "gangster-type" weapons listed in the law: sawed-off shotguns, sawed-off rifles, machine guns, and silencers. In addition, the act set very strict rules on the purchasing and licensing of such weapons. Purchasers of weapons had to undergo a background check by the

Federal Bureau of Investigation (FBI), submit their photographs, and provide full fingerprinting. Each weapon purchased under the law had to be registered.

The firearms industry played a key role in shaping the law. The Roosevelt administration had originally intended to include a plan for the registration of all handguns for a one-dollar fee but dropped the idea when gun manufacturers objected to it. As a result, the phrase "all weaponry" was removed from the registration component and replaced by the words "machine guns and sawed-off shotguns."

The Nye Committee

Political developments in the 1930s also contributed to the backlash against the firearms industry. The difficulty with manufacturing guns is to constantly find new people who want to buy them. Between 1900 and 1935, with the exception of World War I, the United States was technically at peace. This made for slim chances to get rich by making firearms for the U.S. military. Small army budgets led to small orders, yet the Ordnance Department still demanded exceedingly high quality standards. American firearms manufacturers continued to look overseas for markets.

By the 1930s, a majority of Americans were convinced that the U.S. entry into World War I had been a huge mistake. As the Nazis rose to power in Germany, and Japan invaded China, groups ranging from the Socialist Party to the American Legion began complaining about the power of arms manufacturers to influence foreign policy. The result was a Senate investigation known as the Nye Committee hearings, from 1934 to 1936, led by Senator Gerald Nye, a progressive Republican from North Dakota. During the hearings, some U.S. senators claimed that American munitions makers, "merchants of death" to their detractors, had actually helped cause World War I.

The most sensational disclosures of the Nye Committee concerned the international activities of arms and ammunitions makers such as Colt and Smith & Wesson, who had been selling guns in foreign countries for decades. The committee found that "almost without exception, the American munitions companies investigated have at times resorted to such unusual approaches, questionable favors and commissions...as to constitute, in effect, a form of bribery of foreign governmental officials or of their close friends in order to secure business."

For example, a Colt sales agent in Peru, after unloading a huge armament order, boasted to the Peruvians that he would sell "double the amount, and more modern, to the Chilean Government." Firearms manufacturers sold to foreign governments whether they were at peace or war. When a limited number of a weapon, such as machine guns, was available, arms manufacturers forced Bolivia into ordering them on the threat that unless it acted quickly, Paraguay would get them. Firearms sales agents in South America took the attitude that killing backcountry indigenous peoples with airplanes, bombs, and machine guns was simply a chance to sell a product, and "we must make the most of the opportunity."

The Nye Committee declared these actions of munitions makers to be "highly unethical, a discredit to American business, and an unavoidable reflection upon

FAST FACT

A Colt foreign sales agent testified that the whole process of selling firearms abroad "brought into play the most despicable side of human nature; lies, deceit, hypocrisy, greed, and graft occupying a most prominent part in the transactions."

North Dakota senator Gerald Nye reviews a report at a munitions hearing in January 1935. Nye headed a committee that investigated the sometimes shocking and unethical practices of American munitions manufacturers, such as the promotion of violence in foreign countries as a way to sell weapons.

those American governmental agencies which have unwittingly aided in the transactions so contaminated." The committee, noting that the United States already produced half of its required guns and ammunition in government-owned arsenals, recommended government ownership of all weapons-producing plants. This radical idea, however, was derailed by the massive need for firearms in World War II and not proposed again after 1945.

The Garand M-1 Semiautomatic Rifle

> **FAST FACT**
>
> John Garand received no more than his government salary for the M-1 and many other technical improvements that he designed for weapons. During World War II, Congress rejected a bill that would have awarded him $100,000 and gave him a medal instead.

Like Thomas Blanchard in another century, John Garand liked to tinker with machines. As a boy, he patented several inventions, including a machine that would automatically wind the bobbins used in cotton mills. In 1919, at age twenty, he came to the Springfield Armory and eventually rose to the position of chief civilian engineer. In 1924, Garand designed the first workable semiautomatic rifle, the M-1, which was adopted by the U.S. Army in 1936 and the U.S. Marine Corps in 1940, after years of grueling tests. It was often known as the Garand rifle, after its inventor.

The .30-caliber M-1 was a vast improvement over the M1903 Springfield rifle, the Army's previous standard issue firearm. The M-1 was clip-fed, gas-operated, and weighed less than 10 pounds (4.5 kilograms). Its workings were simple enough that it rarely jammed. When a bullet left the barrel, it uncovered a small hole. Compressed gases behind the bullet rushed through a port to a piston and drove it back against the operating rod. These gases rotated the bolt to unlock it and then pushed it back to open the rifle and eject the cartridge case. A recoil spring then closed the bolt and placed a fresh cartridge into position to fire when the trigger was pulled again.

As a semiautomatic weapon, the M-1 fired more than twice as fast as the M1903 Springfield. In fact, the rate of fire was limited only by how fast a soldier could load the eight-round clips of ammunition into the weapon; the clip was automatically ejected after firing the last cartridge. The M-1 also had less recoil than the Springfield, allowing

new soldiers to fire more accurately with a shorter period of training. World War II general George Patton said, "I consider the M-1 the greatest weapon ever made...the most deadly rifle in the world." The first production M-1 rolled off the Springfield assembly lines in July 1937, just in time for World War II. In twenty years, more than 4.5 million M-1s were made at the Springfield Armory.

General Douglas MacArthur, commander of U.S. forces in the Pacific in World War II, reported glowingly on the M-1 to the Ordnance Department: "Under combat conditions [in the Philippines] it operated with no mechanical defects and when used in foxholes did not develop stoppages from dust or dirt. It has been in almost constant action for as much as a week without cleaning or lubrication." The M-1 was the standard weapon of the U.S. Army and Marine Corps during World War II and the Korean War (1950–1953).

The inventor of the M-1 semiautomatic rifle, John Garand, is pictured with his children Janice and Richard in the 1950s, twenty years after the M-1's adoption by the U.S. Army.

Firearms and the
Military-Industrial Complex

Between 1900 and 1930, except for the World War I years of 1917 and 1918, the United States had spent less than 1 percent of its gross national product (GNP) for military purposes. World War II changed this; factories around the nation geared their production to wartime needs after the Japanese attack on Pearl Harbor in 1941. For example, Smith & Wesson virtually ceased gun production for the civilian market, instead churning out more than 1.1 million military and police revolvers.

After World War II ended, however, the U.S. military did not demobilize. For the first time in its history, the United States committed itself to maintaining an enormous peacetime army and providing it with the best weaponry that money could buy. In 1961, even though the United States was technically at peace, Cold War defense spending reached $47 billion—half of all federal spending and almost 10 percent of the GNP. In President Dwight Eisenhower's farewell address in 1961, he warned, "This conjunction of an immense military establishment and a large arms industry is new in the American experience. We must guard

In his farewell speech of 1961, when he left office, President Dwight Eisenhower warned Americans of the potential for misplaced power within what he called the military-industrial complex that had been established at the end of World War II. Eisenhower, elected to two terms as president in the 1950s, is shown here in 1960.

against the acquisition of unwarranted influence...by the military-industrial complex. The potential for the disastrous rise of misplaced power exists and will persist."

Firearms were now only a minor part of defense spending, compared to aircraft, nuclear weapons, and armored vehicles, but the award or denial of a government contract could now make or break a firearms company. For example, the profitability of Colt moved up and down like a roller coaster, with sales and earnings extremely dependent on government orders. These increased sharply during the Korean War and collapsed immediately afterward. Colt revived itself with the M-16 in the 1960s and then careened toward bankruptcy when it lost the contract in 1988. Servicing the U.S. military market became an alluring if perilous route for American firearms firms.

John Browning and the BAR

Automatic weapons fire more than one round with a single depression of the trigger. Several attempts, such as the use of the so-called Pedersen device, had been made to modify the World War I M1903 Springfield rifle into a primitive form of automatic weapon. Most of these designs were unworkable.

John Moses Browning received the first of his hundreds of firearm patents at age twenty-four. The next year, he established an arms factory. In 1883, Browning joined forces with Winchester, and for the next nineteen years, he produced many innovations that helped make Winchester's repeating rifles the most popular in the United States. In 1902, however, Browning broke with Winchester and began collaborating more closely with Fabrique Nationale (FN), a Belgian firm established in 1889. In 1917, working for FN, Browning patented the Browning automatic rifle (BAR), one of the first truly automatic rifles. It was also known as a light machine gun or machine rifle. The BAR was mounted on a bipod, had a shoulder stock, and was magazine-fed. It could fire more than 500 rounds a minute with an effective range of almost 500 yards (450 meters). The BAR was used briefly in 1918 and more extensively in World War II and the Korean War. However, it weighed almost 20 pounds (9 kilograms)—it was not light enough to be used as a standard infantry weapon.

The M-16

During the Cold War—a war of ideas between the United States and the Soviet Union (present-day Russia) for influence around the world, which lasted until the early 1990s—U.S. Army research revealed that most battlefield gunshot deaths occurred at less than 110 yards (100 meters) and were just as likely to occur from random firing as from careful aiming. The Defense Department concluded that a new rifle was needed: one that could produce a hail of lead and be operated by any soldier or draftee, even one who had no experience aiming a gun. In 1957, the U.S. Army asked the Armalite Division of Fairchild Aircraft to develop such a rifle. Eugene Stoner, a designer at Armalite, created a prototype, but the first AR-15s had reliability and accuracy problems. In 1959, Fairchild sold all rights for this design to Colt; Stoner moved to Colt, and the company put all its resources behind the rifle. It was rewarded in 1963 when Colt received government contracts for more than 100,000 M-16s, which were a renamed and modified version of the AR-15 rifles. Three years later, the U.S. Army awarded Colt a $90 million contract for more than 800,000 M-16 rifles.

In 1967, the M-16 was officially adopted as the standard "U.S. Rifle, 5.56mm, M16A1." The rifle weighed less than 8 pounds (3.6 kilograms) and fired a terrifying 650 to 750 rounds a minute. It was accurate to 500 yards (450 meters) when handheld and 800 yards (720 meters) when mounted. Other nations also developed weapons of this type, such as the Russian AK-47 Kalashnikov automatic rifle and the Israeli Uzi submachine gun. One of the key advantages of the M-16, however, was its tremendous versatility. It was constructed so that it was

easy to exchange component parts and adapt the weapon
to many different barrel lengths, weights, and calibers.

The M-16 has proven to be reliable and accurate, but
the early models often jammed in combat when they first
appeared on battlefields in the Vietnam War (1964–1975)
in November 1965. Colt had erroneously promoted the
rifles as "low maintenance," so soldiers were provided with
no cleaning supplies or weapons-care training. After one
battle, an American soldier wrote home, "believe it or not,
you know what killed most of us? Our own rifle. Before we
left Okinawa, [we] were all issued this new rifle, the M16.
Practically everyone of our dead was found with his rifle
torn down next to him where he had been trying to fix it."
A newspaper reporter published pictures of the incident
and caused a great scandal in the United States.
A congressional subcommittee investigated the problem in
1967, and most of the problems were solved by 1970.

At least a dozen large companies in America, such as
Armalite, Bushmaster, Hesse, Les Baer, Olympic, Colt, and

The M-16 rifle, adopted by the military in 1967, has now replaced the M1903 Springfield rifle, in service for thirty-three years, as the weapon used the longest by the military.

Wilson Combat, manufacture M-16s for the civilian and law enforcement markets. Some smaller companies assemble M-16–type rifles from components made by major manufacturers. M-16–type rifles are also manufactured outside the United States, most notably in Canada and China. In 1988, Colt suffered a disastrous blow when the American branch of FN, now known as FN Herstal, became the key supplier of M16A2 rifles to the U.S. Department of Defense. In 1999, however, the U.S. government once again contracted with Colt for 32,000 M-16 rifles, as well as for updating another 88,000 M-16s, helping to revive the company.

The guns of the M-16 family are still the basic weapons of the U.S. infantry. They are also widely used by American police departments and even foreign military groups. Because the United States has not faced a large-scale security threat that has required a completely new standard-issue weapon, the M-16 continues to soldier on. It has now broken the service-life record for longevity previously set by the M1903 Springfield rifle (thirty-three years), and there are currently no plans to replace it.

The Rise of Semiautomatic Pistols

The semiautomatic pistol first appeared at the beginning of the twentieth century. Although it was initially designed as a military weapon, it is now the most popular type of handgun, especially for self-defense and target shooting. Although these pistols use gas pressure from the fired cartridge to reload themselves after every shot (until the magazine is exhausted), it is still necessary to make a separate pull of the trigger for every shot. Most types of semiautomatic pistols use a magazine to feed ammunition through the hollow handgrip into the firing chamber. They can be divided into *blowbacks* and *breechlocks*, depending on their method of reloading. The semiautomatic pistol generally reloads faster than a revolver, but because the mechanism is more complex, a semiautomatic is more likely to jam.

Hugo Borchardt, an American inventor working in Germany, designed the first practical semiautomatic handgun in 1894. The Borchardt was the ancestor of German models such as the Mauser and the Luger. In the United States, the ever-present John Browning designed the first self-loading pistols, manufactured in Europe by FN and in America by Colt. The .45 Colt 1911 was adopted by the U.S. military and remained in service for more than seventy years. Firearms firms such as Colt, Beretta, Browning, Glock, H&K, SIG/Sauer, and Walther now make the most popular American semiautomatic pistols.

Semiautomatic pistols have replaced revolvers in military use and also are making headway in police forces. In 1974, most handguns sold in the United States were still revolvers, but self-loading pistols were the majority in 2000. There is some dispute as to the reason for this change. Revolvers are currently used mostly in personal self-defense and target practice, but even for these purposes, semiautomatics are replacing them.

The rise of semiautomatic pistols changed the nature of gun sales in America. Handguns represented only about one-

A Glock 9mm handgun allegedly used in a 1999 murder is shown in an evidence photo. Semiautomatic pistols like this make up the majority of handguns sold in America for civilian use. Handguns in general are the preferred weapons for both self-defense and crime.

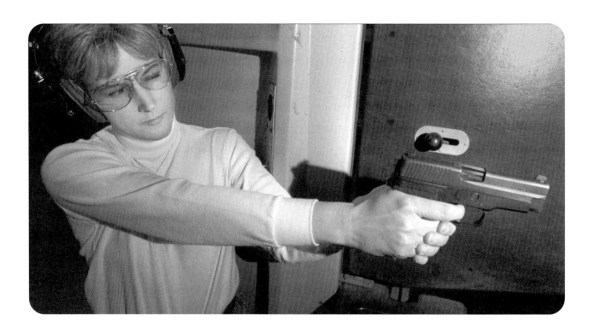

Gun enthusiasts, like this employee at a shooting range in Connecticut, would disagree that the firearms industry has played a role in the increase in crime in the United States and that it has had a negative impact on the quality of American life. This woman said she purchased her gun after a rash of carjackings in her city.

fifth of all guns purchased in America in the 1950s; until 1967, handgun sales had never totaled more than 700,000 in any year. From 1982 to 1993, however, Americans bought 50 million guns, of which about 20 million were handguns; handgun sales exceeded 2 million every year between 1979 and 1982. Approximately one-third of the guns owned by Americans are handguns; they continue to be the preferred weapon for both self-defense and crime.

The Rise of Gun Control

Until the 1960s, the firearms industry did not usually play a major role in American politics or culture. Occasional flurries of interest in the industry quickly passed. The Nye Committee and the National Firearms Act of 1934 marked the high point of federal control of gun use in the United States; the extremely weak Federal Firearms Act of 1938 produced no more than 100 arrests per year. After World War II, 9 million veterans returned to the United States, many with a new interest in firearms. Hunting and target shooting surged in popularity, but the issue of the role of guns in American life attracted little attention.

After 1960, the situation began to change. Surplus army weapons resulting from World War II, the Korean

War, and the Cold War began to flood the United States. The crime rate began to rise, peaking in the late 1980s and early 1990s. Television news shows constantly reported on crime and gun violence because they were dramatic and easy to cover. Increased political violence in the 1960s, in the form of assassinations and race riots, caused many Americans to view the firearms industry as having a negative impact on the quality of American life. Gun manufacturers were forced to operate in a climate in which the value of their very existence was questioned.

Changes in the Gun Industry

The great names in the American firearms industry—Winchester, Colt, Remington, Smith & Wesson—were originally family firms. With the exception of O.F. Mossberg (founded in 1919), however, almost none of these old firearms companies remain family owned and operated. The huge fluctuations in the demand for firearms have made independent production almost impossible to sustain. Weapons manufacturers face unusually difficult problems; they need to rapidly increase production and the number of workers when America goes to war, but then sharply reduce both when the war is over, or promote weapons sales to the general public. The solution has usually been to start producing products other than guns. For instance, at one time or another, Remington made typewriters, sewing machines, clothing, cash registers, and various tools and utensils. In the process, many firearms companies have become major or minor parts of other corporations—sometimes foreign-owned multinational corporations.

Smith & Wesson is a good example. For over a century, from 1854 to 1965, the firm had been family owned. In the next forty years, however, it changed hands numerous times: It was sold to Bangor Punta Corporation in 1965, purchased by Lear Siegler Corporation in 1984, and sold again only two years later to Forstmann Little. That company, however, bought Lear Siegler for its automotive and aerospace industries and had no desire at all to produce firearms. It sold Smith & Wesson as quickly as possible to Tomkins of London, a huge multinational corporation with only a minor interest in manufacturing handguns. In 2002, Saf-T-Hammer, an Arizona firearms company, purchased Smith & Wesson for $20 million. As part of the acquisition, Saf-T-Hammer changed its name to the Smith & Wesson Holding Corporation.

Winchester, the manufacturer of the legendary rifles and carbines used by millions of Americans for recreational shooting and hunting, is no longer American-owned. In 1989, the company—previously known as the Browning/U.S. Repeating Arms Company—was taken over by FN. FN's Herstal group—under the brand names FN Herstal, Browning, and Winchester—designs, manufactures, and distributes a wide range of firearms for defense, law enforcement, hunting, and marksmanship. The multinational corporation is headquartered in Liege, Belgium, but also has offices in nine other European countries, North America, and Asia.

Colt, the most famous name in American firearms, remained in family hands until 1901. In 1955, Colt was purchased by the Penn-Texas Corporation, one of the nation's first conglomerates. (A *conglomerate* is a huge corporation made up of very different businesses.) In 1990, the declining company was purchased by a group of private investors allied with the firm's union employees and the state of Connecticut. This did not prevent Colt from going bankrupt in 1992; in May 1994, the company closed the world-famous but antiquated Hartford Armory and moved out to West Hartford. A new group of private investors purchased the company in 1994, and it has recently been making small strides toward profitability, reclaiming some government contracts that it had lost.

Some historic names in American firearms have been reborn simply because entrepreneurs believed that the nostalgic appeal would help sell the product. Derringers are made by American Derringer Corporation, but the company, founded in 1980, has no relationship to the nineteenth-century company other than the gun design. In 1974, Robert Reese bought the rights to the famous name of "Springfield Armory" and began producing military and civilian rifles from a factory in Geneseo, Illinois. The company has absolutely nothing to do with the historic armory, which closed in 1968, yet still advertises itself (technically correctly) as "the oldest name in American firearms."

Bill Ruger

One firearms firm that has successfully endured during the last fifty years is Sturm, Ruger & Company—currently the largest arms manufacturer in the United States. William Ruger, its founder, was born in 1916 in Brooklyn, New York. He developed a passion for guns at the age of twelve when his father gave him a rifle. In college, he converted an empty room at the University of North Carolina into a machine shop and developed the initial designs for what eventually became a light machine gun for the army. Ruger helped invent and patent dozens of models of sporting firearms and was widely recognized as America's greatest gun designer before his death in 2002.

In 1949, Ruger teamed with Alexander Sturm to establish the Sturm, Ruger Company. After Sturm's death in 1951, the company produced more types of sporting firearms than any other firm in the world, and it has manufactured more than 20 million guns in the last half-century. The first firearm that Ruger introduced in 1949, a .22-caliber target pistol, was "the first gun" of many Americans and remains one of the most popular American target pistols. Sturm, Ruger manufactures its guns in Newport, New Hampshire, and Prescott, Arizona; the company is one of the only firearms companies publicly traded on the New York Stock Exchange.

Despite his reputation as America's greatest firearms designer since John Browning, some gun owners considered Ruger a traitor when he began supporting gun

> **FAST FACT**
>
> By restricting magazines to no more than ten rounds, Ruger's proposal had the indirect effect of sparking the interest of gun buyers and designers of small, easy-to-conceal handguns.

The Sturm, Ruger .22-caliber target pistol has been one of the most popular target pistols sold since its introduction in 1949. This photograph shows both a basic target pistol (bottom), costing around $300, and a fully equipped model, costing around $2,000.

control measures. He told a national television audience, "No honest man needs more than 10 rounds in any gun" and "I never meant for simple civilians to have my 20 or 30 round mags or my folding stock" and "I see nothing wrong with waiting periods." In 1989, Ruger sent a letter to every member of Congress which claimed that "a simple, complete and unequivocal ban on large capacity magazines" would eliminate the difficulty of defining the terms *assault rifle* and *semiautomatic rifle*. "A single amendment to Federal firearms laws," stated the firearms entrepreneur, "could effectively implement these objectives." Congress accepted this argument when it passed the assault weapons ban in 1994.

The American Firearms Industry in 2000

In the 1800s, the firearms industry pioneered the use of machines in manufacturing. This emphasis on technology took the production of guns out of the hands of individual artisans and placed it in the hands of large companies with factories. Like many other old manufacturing industries in America (such as automobile production), the production of firearms has become increasingly concentrated in a few major companies. For some gun types, there is very little competition. For example, two companies—Smith & Wesson and Sturm, Ruger—account for 98 percent of all American revolver production. Four manufacturers—Remington Arms, O.F. Mossberg, Harrington & Richardson (founded in 1871), and U.S. Repeating Arms—manufacture 92 percent of all shotguns produced in the United States. A wider range of companies—more than thirty in all—manufacture pistols, led by Smith & Wesson; Sturm, Ruger; and Beretta.

Again, as in many old manufacturing industries, firearms imports have increased while the domestic production and export of American-manufactured guns have decreased. In particular, Beretta, an Italian firearms firm that dates back to 1526, has had great success selling handguns in America. Many police and sheriff departments use Beretta pistols, as does the U.S. Border Patrol. The U.S. Army has even adopted the Beretta 92 semiautomatic pistol.

An Uncertain Future

Most American gun producers are privately owned companies. A few—most famously Sturm, Ruger—have tried to raise investment capital by selling stock to the public. Several large, publicly traded corporations manufacture firearms (such as Olin, which owns U.S. Repeating Arms) along with other products. Because privately owned companies do not have to reveal their earnings, it is difficult to say if firearms manufacturers make a great deal of money, some money, or any money at all. Profits vary from company to company; Bill Ruger, who became quite wealthy, famously stated, "We have a little moneymaking machine here," but other companies have not fared as well. One analyst claims that the U.S. firearms industry enjoys "incredible profitability," while another characterizes profits as "modest." Colt's recent bankruptcy is surely a sign that the manufacture of guns is not a sure way to financial success.

The firearms industry has to face the likely continued decline of hunting and also deal with the problem of market saturation. Most people who want to own guns probably already own them. This means that the industry has to search for people who do not already own guns or develop new features to make people buy more modern models, such as so-called personal or "smart guns."

The firearms industry has tried to pitch guns to women (who are underrepresented as owners) and to drum up interest in shooting sports among young people. Nonetheless, handgun sales peaked in 1993 at about 2.8 million guns. In 2000, only about 1.2 million were sold, the lowest total since 1981. *Shooting Industry,* a leading gun industry publication, noted that "the industry will continue to experience changes as it struggles to compete with a recreation-saturated society." It remains to be seen whether the terrorist attacks on September 11, 2001, and the resulting widespread anxiety among Americans will translate into a boom for the firearms industry.

American firearms companies have also had a difficult time because many people are reluctant to invest money in such an unstable industry. Money spent on research and development has not been an American strength in recent years; the number of patents has remained fairly flat, and most inventors seem to be individual hobbyists. The public debate about gun control and the use of lawsuits to obtain civil damages from gun manufacturers have created an uncertain environment. The gun industry in the United States remains caught in a tough position; it provides a popular product that is adored by many Americans, yet viewed with extreme hostility by others.

CHAPTER 5

Safer Guns?

By design, firearms manufacturers produce a product that kills people and destroys things. Guns are used mainly for hunting, sports, and self-defense, but a small minority of them are also involved in accidents, suicides, and crime. In 2000, more than 500,000 victims of serious violent crimes such as rape, robbery, and assault in the United States stated that they faced an offender with a gun. Of the 16,765 murders in America in 2000, two-thirds were committed with firearms. In addition, guns sometimes kill people accidentally. In 2000, more than 700 fatal gun accidents were reported in the United States; almost a quarter of the people accidentally killed by guns were under the age of eighteen.

In the last forty years, a large number of Americans have concluded both that guns need to be made safer and that there are just too many guns in circulation. A number of remedies have been suggested that pertain specifically to the firearms industry. Gun manufacturers have been asked to develop "smart guns," add internal trigger locks, take ballistic fingerprints, and subject guns to national consumer safety standards. Some critics have suggested a one-gun-a-month limit for handgun purchases. Any of these changes would affect the profitability of the firearms industry; a one-a-month limit on gun purchases would restrict sales, while safety features would raise the cost of firearms without boosting sales in any meaningful way.

Gun manufacturers rely on certain arguments that apply to almost all safety proposals. They object that guns are inherently dangerous, that their benefit to society as weapons of self-defense outweighs their liabilities, and that required safety features will raise the cost of guns and price poor people out of the firearms market. Most importantly, manufacturers believe that all attempts to improve the safety record of guns are actually part of a plot to bring on measures that will eventually lead to gun confiscation. This is known as a "slippery slope" argument; any and every first gun safety step must be opposed because, otherwise, it would begin the long and unstoppable slide to dictatorship in America.

Although the debate over gun safety directly concerns the firearms industry, manufacturers have attempted to stay in the background; they did not even hire a Washington, D.C., lobbyist until 1989. In general, firearms companies have left the political wrangling to gun advocacy groups such as the National Rifle Association (NRA). The NRA has taken the lead in speaking for the firearms industry on safety legislation by lobbying politicians, forming political action committees, and funding public relations campaigns. Although the NRA benefits from a close relationship with gun companies, its strength rests with its highly motivated mass membership that exists completely independently of gun manufacturers.

Smart Guns

Perhaps the most intriguing suggestion for twenty-first-century gun design is the development of so-called smart guns. These personalized guns are weapons that incorporate

An Australian gun owner shows his "smart gun." This four-barreled gun can fire a deadly four bullets at once, but it can be activated only by its owner. A handful of smart guns exist, but the technology for their full-scale manufacture has not yet been developed.

the latest technology so that they can be fired only by their owners. If it were possible to construct such a gun, it would reduce accidental firearms injuries and also gun suicides by unauthorized users, such as young family members, by making it impossible for them to operate such guns.

Smart guns would be safer than firearms with trigger locks because the technology would not be removable; the gun would automatically be stored in a locked position. More than 500,000 guns are stolen from homes each year, but if they were smart guns, the thieves would not be able to use them to commit other crimes. During the 1990s, fifty-seven police officers were killed when their own weapons were grabbed from them. If smart guns could be developed, law enforcement officers would not get shot when their own guns were grabbed and used against them in a fight.

The question is whether the technology exists, or could ever exist, to make smart guns commercially possible. In 2000, the U.S. Department of Justice announced a partnership with gun companies Smith & Wesson and FN Manufacturing to see if it was possible to produce a workable smart gun. Taurus International, another leading gun maker, began working with the New Jersey Institute of Technology in 2001 to develop a smart gun that would use sensors in the gun's grip wired to a microchip inside the gun. The owner would have his or her grip programmed at a gun shop or police range by practice-firing the gun. The chip would then "remember" an individual owner's handgrip and prevent the gun from firing if anyone else attempted to use it. "It's going to be a monumental challenge to achieve a level of reliability in order for this to be usable technology," said a Taurus representative, "but knowing it will eventually happen, we feel better being a partner in that development instead of waiting on the sidelines for it to be handed to us."

Many gun owners' organizations oppose the development of smart guns. They believe that the technology will probably never exist to commercially produce absolutely foolproof personalized guns. "Nothing has been devised yet that is fully reliable," said a representative from Sturm, Ruger. "There is zero room for error here," he said. "If you swipe your ATM card and it doesn't read it, do it again. But if you reach for your gun to defend yourself and it doesn't recognize your identification, you don't get a second chance." The cost of smart guns is also a concern for firearms manufacturers. If the price is too high, poorer families will be unable to afford them, and this will cut into profits. As always, some gun enthusiasts warn that any governmental requirement of smart guns will lead to the confiscation and destruction of "non-smart" guns. An NRA spokesman stated, "When used by the gun prohibition groups and their political allies, the term [smart guns] is a euphemism for 'gun prohibition.'"

> **FAST FACT**
>
> In 2000, more than 16,000 Americans used guns to commit suicide; 754 were age eighteen or younger.

New Jersey's Smart Gun Law

Because of the reluctance of gun manufacturers such as Glock to invest in the development of personalized guns, some states have tried to offer them some incentive. In December 2002, New Jersey became the first state to pass smart gun legislation. The law will eventually require all new handguns bought in New Jersey to have some mechanism that allows only their owners to fire them. This law obviously cannot take effect immediately, because the technology is still being developed. However, the law states that all New Jersey handguns must have smart gun technology within three years after the state's attorney general declares that a smart gun prototype is safe and commercially available. Supporters of the law claim that it would prevent accidental gun injuries, suicides, and gun thefts. New Jersey governor James McGreevey stated, "This is commonsense legislation. There are safety requirements on cars, on toys. It's clearly time we have safety regulations on handguns."

Opponents of the New Jersey law argued that it makes no sense to pass legislation on technology that doesn't exist yet; the best fingerprint recognition system currently works only about 80 percent of the time. A representative of the Association of New Jersey Rifle and Pistol Clubs noted that "no technology is foolproof. Anyone who has a computer knows how many times it crashes."

Ballistic Fingerprinting

A 9mm semiautomatic pistol, along with its magazine, bullet, and bullet casing, is displayed at a California forensics laboratory. Both Maryland and New York have passed laws that require weapons to be test-fired before they are sold, a practice known as ballistic fingerprinting.

Bullets and shell casings fired from a handgun contain unique individual markings. These markings, like fingerprints, can be used to link a specific handgun with a specific crime that was committed with that gun. To a degree, police with sophisticated computer equipment can use these markings to decide if a bullet or shell casing was fired from one particular firearm. Supporters of ballistic fingerprinting want all handguns to be test-fired before they are sold. Each gun's "fingerprints" would then be entered into a computer, and experienced firearms examiners would be able to help law enforcement officers use the information when a crime is committed.

In the late 1990s, New York and Maryland passed laws that require new handguns to be test-fired before they are sold. The used bullets or shell casings are then collected and classified. Police rarely find the actual handgun used in a gun crime, but they often turn up bullets and shell casings. Ballistic fingerprinting would theoretically increase the ability of law enforcement to link guns with gun crimes, increasing the chance of finding and locking up criminals. Smith & Wesson and Glock, two major firearms manufacturers, are currently installing a system to produce digital images of ballistic material for all handguns produced. Each company will maintain its own database that will be accessible to law enforcement.

The BATF and IBIS

Federal law enforcement agencies already use ballistic fingerprinting through a system operated by the Bureau of Alcohol, Tobacco, and Firearms (BATF) called the National Integrated Ballistic Information Network. The network connects police with the computerized Integrated Ballistic Identification System (IBIS), also run by the BATF and established in its current form in 2000. By 2003, IBIS had accumulated more than 120,000 ballistic fingerprint images on file from guns and bullet fragments found at crime scenes around the United States. Firearms examiners have used IBIS to generate more than 5,000 matches of bullets or casings recovered from different crime scenes. At present, the police can compare bullets and cartridge casings found at different crime scenes, but they cannot identify the specific guns that produced those bullets or casings.

After a sniper murdered ten people and terrorized the Washington, D.C., area in 2002, gun control advocates pushed for a national computerized system for tracing bullets and shell casings to the guns that fired them. This system would require all firearms manufacturers to test-fire new guns before distributing them to stores. The information detailing the markings left on bullets by each weapon would then be scanned into IBIS. In theory, a national ballistic fingerprinting database would allow investigators who have found a bullet at the scene of a crime to enter the data about the bullet's markings into a computer and then quickly retrieve possible gun matches. This information could lead them to the gun's buyer and possibly the perpetrator of the crime.

For example, in one New York City double homicide, the police department had almost no evidence to work with besides the bullet shells and casings from the crime scene. After exhausting all other leads, detectives took those shells and casings to the NYPD ballistics lab to be scanned into IBIS. The ballistics lab connected the gun used in the double homicide to one used three months later in an armed robbery. Based on this match, a man was arrested and convicted of both crimes. Without ballistic fingerprinting, this case might never have been solved.

Opposition to Ballistic Fingerprinting

There is considerable doubt if the technology exists to make ballistic fingerprinting a reliable or even workable system. Unlike fingerprints, the markings from bullets and shell casings can be altered. A firearm barrel and firing pin may be altered, replaced, or deformed by normal use or even intentionally falsified with new markings. If ballistic fingerprints can easily be changed, the whole system is impractical. Ballistic fingerprinting in Maryland has yet to have any impact on criminal convictions, despite the fingerprinting of thousands of guns since January 2000.

Many opponents of ballistic fingerprinting believe that it is actually a registration system for handguns in disguise. They claim that the system would give police a list of all handgun owners, which could possibly be the first step to confiscation of all handguns. Although fingerprinting would apply only to newly manufactured firearms, the NRA predicts that "anti-gun activists would soon demand that the 'loopholes' in the system be closed and that all of the more than 200 million privately owned firearms in America be surrendered to authorities for 'fingerprinting.'" Yet, the NRA insists, nothing would prevent a criminal from using a stolen gun or altering a firearm before using it in a crime, which would make any bullet or cartridge case comparisons absolutely useless.

Opponents also object that instituting the record-keeping necessary for ballistic fingerprinting would be an expensive waste of time. Each state (or the entire nation) would have to develop and maintain a large database of spent bullets and cartridges, most of which would never be used in crime. A study by the California Department of Justice, released in 2003, concluded that the current technology was unreliable and that cataloging the ballistic fingerprints of every firearm in the nation's most populous state would be impractical.

In October 2002, the NRA declared that ballistic fingerprinting was "flawed, unworkable and infringes on the rights of tens of millions of law-abiding Americans." President George W. Bush's administration agreed, but, under popular pressure to do something after the Washington, D.C., sniper attacks, stated that it would allow the BATF to review the issue. Politicians had to take some account of polls that demonstrated widespread support, even among gun owners, for ballistic fingerprinting.

Two sample bullets from the same 9mm semiautomatic pistol are displayed to show the similarities in their markings or "fingerprints," left by the action of their firing from the same gun. A California study concluded in 2003 that ballistic fingerprinting was impractical and probably not worth the effort and expense it would take to implement.

Trigger Locks

In 1999, guns were involved in approximately 700 accidental deaths and 9,100 unintentional injuries across the United States. Surveys seem to show that more than one-third of American households keep firearms in the home or car and that more than 20 percent of these guns are left loaded and unlocked.

A *trigger lock* is a type of safety lock that can prevent a gun's trigger from firing by accident. These locks are an inexpensive way to prevent guns kept in the home from being operated by unauthorized users, such as unsupervised children. There are several different external styles available, including locks that work with keys, combination locks, and alarms. The most common is a vinyl-covered steel cable—something like a small version of a bicycle cable lock—that can be placed through the chamber on a pistol, revolver, or rifle. Although these locks cost about twenty dollars each, some programs, such as Project HomeSafe, run by the National Shooting Sports Foundation (NSSF), donate them to cities that then give them to law enforcement agencies to distribute for free.

Because there are no federal standards for trigger locks, their quality varies widely. In 2001, the Consumer Product Safety Commission (CPSC) tested thirty-two locks. It found that all but two of them could be defeated by children who could open them without a key and, in some instances, with only a paper clip. Some guns with locks that make the trigger inaccessible still allowed the gun to fire. The same year, the NSSF agreed to recall 400,000 of the free (but defective) locks that it had given away as part of its Project HomeSafe campaign. Ironically, the NSSF had launched that campaign in the first place to avoid any legislative efforts that would force gun manufacturers to equip all new products with trigger locks.

Some gun safety advocates support laws that would require internal trigger locks built into every handgun. These advocates believe that internal locks would reduce unintentional firearm deaths and suicides. "I think if we

had such a law in 1998, my son might still be living," stated Carole Price. Her thirteen-year-old son John was killed four years ago when another teen playing with a gun accidentally shot him. "With the external locks, you can forget," Price said. "But [with] the internal locks, you can only use [the gun] by unlocking it."

The Case Against Trigger Locks

Representatives of the firearms industry are more skeptical. They believe that the locks will increase the price of the guns and probably won't make a difference in reducing suicides, accidents, or thefts involving firearms. "A kid, if he wants to, will figure out how it works," stated one opponent of mandatory trigger locks; money would be better spent in firearms education programs. In addition, gun manufacturers dispute the importance of

State representatives in Florida take part in a 2000 press conference aimed at focusing attention on the state's slowness in passing gun safety legislation. Maryland is the only state that has passed a law requiring built-in trigger locks on all guns. The law, which was passed in 2000, applied to all guns purchased after 2003.

To allay the concern of firearms manufacturers that mandatory trigger locks will increase the price of guns, some law enforcement agencies distribute locks free of charge. Locks similar to this one were distributed free in Ocean County, New Jersey, in 1999.

fatal firearm accidents, especially among children. In 2000, only ninety-eight children under age fifteen died as the result of gun accidents; although this is a tragic number, manufacturers argue that it hardly requires a costly remedy involving million of guns.

A trigger lock might also increase the time that it takes a gun owner to respond to a self-defense emergency. Gun Owners of America (GOA) strongly opposes gun safety locks in principle. The organization points to occasions when crime victims could not defend themselves because they could not get access to guns that they knew how to use. "When it comes to life or death issues," the GOA believes that individuals should take the initiative for their own self-defense and not rely too heavily on the police or the government.

State Action

There is currently no national law requiring trigger locks for firearms or any national safety standard for trigger locks. In 2001, California adopted strict standards for trigger locks sold in that state. The safety device requirement, however, does not apply to law enforcement officers, owners of antique firearms, and people who can demonstrate that they own a gun safe.

In 2000, Maryland's legislature passed a law requiring built-in trigger locks in all new handguns bought in the state after 2003. Maryland was the first state to require internal trigger locks on new handguns—the state has a history of passing strong gun laws. Maryland had already banned assault weapons and "Saturday night specials" and limited handgun purchases to one per person per month. Maryland's governor, Parris Glendening, said, "Gun manufacturers can make safer guns, and they should be required to make safer guns. That's the substantive message."

Even after the law took effect, however, dealers were allowed to sell their existing inventory, as well as used guns without the internal locks. Still, gun dealers complained that the new trigger lock law would reduce their business by 80 percent. At present, most firearms companies don't make guns with internal trigger locks, and they're unlikely to begin just because Maryland passed its own trigger lock law.

One Gun a Month

The U.S. government has conducted several studies that show that areas with strong gun laws, such as New York, California, Maryland, and Chicago, Illinois, are still swamped with handguns. These weapons are bought in large quantities by gun smugglers in states with weak gun laws and transported to large cities where they can be sold illegally for large profits. States like New York and Maryland, which regulate the sale and possession of firearms, are subjected to illegal guns entering their communities from states that do not regulate firearms. For example, one survey in the 1990s reported that more than 90 percent of crime guns recovered in New York City were originally purchased in other states.

FAST FACT

Federal law does not limit the number of guns that a person can buy at any one time. It does, however, require licensed firearms dealers to report the sale of two or more handguns to an unlicensed person within five consecutive business days to the BATF.

"One-gun-a-month" proposals attempt to reduce this illegal interstate gun trafficking by prohibiting a purchaser from buying more than one gun each month, thereby making it difficult for criminals to buy many firearms legally in one state and transport them to another state with stricter gun safety laws for illegal sale. In 1975, South Carolina was the first state to try to stop gun trafficking through this type of measure. The concept became the subject of a national debate in 1993, when Virginia passed a similar law. Before the law, Virginia's gun dealers supplied more than 40 percent of the guns traced to crimes in New York City. Virginia's generally conservative politicians and business leaders supported the law, because they felt that the distinction of being the "firearms supermarket" for the East Coast hurt the state's reputation and economic development. Maryland passed a similar law in 1996.

Studies seem to show that the one-gun-a-month laws work. An analysis of the Virginia law found that the percentage of guns traced back to Virginia gun dealers was reduced by 71 percent for guns recovered in New York and 72 percent for guns recovered in Massachusetts. Polls show considerable popular support among Americans, including law enforcement agents, for limiting handgun purchases to one per month. In March 1999, Los Angeles, California, became the first major city in the United States to pass a one-gun-a-month law. The next month, following the Columbine High School shooting massacre in Colorado, the California legislature passed a one-gun-a-month law for the entire state. This made California the fourth, the largest, and currently the last state to try to stop gun trafficking through this measure.

Guns used in crimes are likely to have been bought as part of multiple sales. The BATF's *Crime Gun Trace Reports* of 1999 studied the origins of more than 60,000 guns used in crimes that year. Handguns sold in multiple sales accounted for 22 percent of all handguns sold and traced to crimes in 1999. Undoubtedly, many more multiple sales were not reported, since only 11 percent of traced crime guns were purchased from federally licensed gun dealers. Handguns with obliterated serial numbers were more than twice as likely as those without obliterated serial numbers to have been acquired in a multiple sale. It would seem that restricting multiple sales of guns is a useful crime prevention strategy.

The Case against Gun Sale Limitations

The chief lobbyist for one gun group called one-gun-a-month laws "an insidious attempt to tell Americans that they do not have a right to the means necessary for self-defense for at least thirty days." He protested the "vicious principle…that it is the prerogative of the government, and not the right of the individual, law-abiding citizen, to determine when he or she needs or wants a particular arm for legitimate purpose." Shooters, like other sports enthusiasts, tend to have more than one gun. A gun dealer noted that "like the tennis player with a closet full of rackets, they are always looking for the newest and latest thing." Why should the government prevent a law-abiding citizen from purchasing as many guns as he or she wants?

The president of a gun control group in Indiana points out a loophole in that state's law requiring background checks for all gun buyers. An AR-15 assault weapon, like the one pictured behind her, was advertised for sale in a newspaper. The seller would have no way to perform the required background check on a prospective buyer, a tempting loophole for someone who might wish to use the gun in a crime.

Opponents of one-gun-a-month laws also point out that such laws are not needed because transporting a gun across state lines and then reselling it without a federal license is already a crime; furthermore, even if the intention is good, one-gun-a-month laws do not work because criminals use other people (known as straw buyers) to make the quantity of purchases that they need.

Some gun owners fear the registration component of one-gun-a-month laws. In order for the police to successfully enforce limits on multiple handgun purchases, retail handgun sales have to be reported to a state or national law enforcement office, and those records are then computerized and maintained for at least thirty days. This seems to give state and national governments more leeway to track and regulate gun ownership.

Safety and the Firearms Industry

Pressure on American gun manufacturers to include safety features or limit the sale of guns typically results from the momentary outrage of the general public following school shootings and sniper attacks. However, firearms manufacturers and gun enthusiasts oppose regulations such as one-gun-a-month laws because they believe that limiting the number of purchases per month is, if not a violation of the Bill of Rights, then a step in that direction. Lobbying groups such as the NRA oppose almost any legislation that mentions the word *guns,* even legislation as seemingly harmless as limiting handgun purchases to twelve a year. They believe that every government limitation on gun ownership is another step down the slippery slope to gun confiscation. Because "slippery slope" arguments depend on a possible event that has not yet occurred (in this case, the confiscation of 200 million guns and the rise of dictatorship in America), they can never be disputed, let alone disproved. In the first decade of the twenty-first century, the debate over gun legislation seems to have reached a logical impasse.

CHAPTER 6

Manufacturer's Product Liability

f a defective product causes someone an injury, that person is allowed to sue the manufacturer in a court of law to collect damages. However, American negligence law (known as *tort law*) also holds that the producers of items can be held responsible for products that are defective in design, regardless of whether or not they malfunction. Beginning in the 1990s, some people began to apply this principle to gun manufacturers. They sued firearms companies for damages resulting from the failure to include possible safety devices that could prevent injuries caused by the foreseeable use or even the foreseeable misuse of guns (for example, if a child found and played with a gun).

Similar lawsuits had been used effectively against the automobile industry to ensure that some safety features were included in all cars. In one of the most famous product liability cases, Ford was held responsible in the 1970s for fires caused by the placement of the gas tank in the Ford Pinto. The gas tank did not cause the car to malfunction, but its poor design posed an unreasonable risk to the passengers, who would be burned to death in the event of a rear-end collision (a foreseeable misuse of the product).

The lawsuits against the gun industry, however, were extremely controversial. Guns, after all, are meant to shoot people (or things). Negligence law also recognizes the importance of responsible individual behavior. Some lawsuits alleged that the gun industry knowingly distributed guns in a reckless fashion, not caring that they could get into the hands of criminals. Yet guns are a legal product; is the firearms industry really responsible for the misuse of its product by a small minority of gun owners?

Consumer Safety Standards

Such safety lawsuits stem from a peculiarity regarding the creation of the Consumer Product Safety Commission (CPSC) by the U.S. Congress in 1972. The CPSC was supposed to test and regulate the production and marketing of American products to make sure that they did not harm the health or safety of consumers. In the final

version of the law that established the CPSC, supporters of the gun industry added a provision that specifically forbade the CPSC or any other national government agency from regulating firearms or ammunition. In 1975, Senator Ted Kennedy, a Democrat of Massachusetts, suggested an amendment giving the CPSC oversight over guns and ammunition, but the Senate crushed it by an overwhelming seventy-five to eleven vote.

Safety features always add to the cost of a product. The CPSC was supposed to work in the interest of the consumer to regulate private businesses driven to cut corners by competition and the desire for profits. Supporters of CPSC regulation of firearms pointed to the success of government regulation of automobiles, which led to improvements in car design and tremendous declines in automobile accident deaths. They claim that, in the same way, subjecting gun manufacturers to safety regulations would be an important step toward preventing accidental gun deaths.

These guns and ammunition supplies were confiscated in Gary, Indiana, in 1999 after police raided the shops that had sold the guns to officers posing as gang members and minors. The city sued the gun shops, as well as some gun manufacturers, claiming negligence. Lawsuits of this type, however, are extremely controversial.

Senator Howard Metzenbaum introduced a bill in Congress in 1998 to allow the Consumer Product Safety Commission (CPSC) to regulate the firearms industry, as it regulates most other consumer industries. The bill failed, however.

At present, however, the federal government cannot require the placement of safety features on firearms. Guns made in the United States are one of the only consumer products (another major exception is tobacco) that are exempt; firearms imported from other countries must meet minimum safety standards.

In recent years, some people have suggested that the government should require the firearms industry to provide uniform quality and safety standards for American-made guns. In 1998, Senator Howard Metzenbaum, Democrat of Ohio, introduced a bill in Congress to have guns regulated by the CPSC. The bill never came close to passing. Metzenbaum blamed the lobbying power of the NRA for the failure to pass the law. He said, "The NRA's position is consistent. They're opposed to any legislation that has the word 'gun' anywhere in it."

The firearms industry and its supporters basically agree with this position. They argue that any law about guns is really part of a plot to regulate guns more strictly or ban guns entirely. Opponents of CPSC regulation claim that any new safety measures might lead to the confiscation of existing handguns that do not meet the safety levels. Gun rights supporters don't think that guns are "unsafe." Instead, they believe that they are dangerous in the wrong hands but quite safe in the right hands.

CPSC Actions

Despite its legal limitations, the CPSC has had some impact on the gun industry. In July 2000, it forced Master Lock of Milwaukee to recall about 750,000 defective trigger locks and provide free replacements to consumers. In February 2001, the CPSC made the NSSF recall the 400,000 locks that it had distributed free of charge to gun owners as part of its Project HomeSafe campaign for safe storage.

In October 2001, the CPSC began a lawsuit against Daisy Manufacturing, seeking the recall of 7.5 million air guns (known as BB guns). The CPSC claimed that at least 15 deaths and 171 serious injuries—80 percent of them of children under sixteen—have been associated with the air guns. The CPSC wanted Daisy to use an automatic safety system; the air guns have a manual one. Daisy refused to recall the weapons, arguing that they had been on sale since September 1972. Both supporters and opponents of CPSC regulation of firearms (BB guns are not firearms) cite the Daisy case as exactly why government oversight of gun manufacturers is or isn't needed. Supporters see a responsible government agency working in the interest of public safety, while opponents see a meddling bureaucracy with the power to confiscate all guns sometime in the future.

> **FAST FACT**
>
> The Daisy recall was pushed by the family of John T. Mahoney. In 1999, the sixteen-year-old Pennsylvania youth was shot in the head by a friend and left in a near vegetative state with severe injuries. Daisy settled a suit with the family for $18 million.

Product-Safety Liability

Because Congress repeatedly failed to pass legislation that would regulate guns or allow the CPSC to oversee gun manufacturers, supporters of gun safety have recently used a controversial tactic borrowed from anticigarette activists. They have begun taking the gun industry to court, claiming that it is legally negligent because it refuses to manufacture guns with sufficient safety features. In addition, the supporters of gun safety argue, developing gun safety technology, such as smart guns, could reduce the number of firearms available in the illegal market by making stolen guns unusable. Because safety equipment adds to the cost of any product, these supporters believe that only lawsuits will force the industry to adopt such technology.

Such lawsuits have often been brought against specific gun manufacturers by the relatives of people who have been accidentally killed by guns. The suits claim that the technology exists, and has existed for many years, to make handguns safer and reduce the number of accidental deaths that occur each year due to firearms. Gun manufacturers could have—and should have—incorporated these available safety features into the design of the gun. Although most of these lawsuits by individuals have been unsuccessful, sympathetic judges, and especially juries, have begun to hold gun manufacturers and gun dealers liable for their products.

The Response of the Firearms Industry

Gun manufacturers respond to lawsuits over gun safety by pointing out that guns, and especially handguns, are designed to kill. If people require a firearm for self-defense, they need to use it quickly. Firearms companies believe that safety features complicate weapons and might even prevent gun owners from responding quickly to an emergency, costing the owners their lives.

Gun manufacturers argue instead that the solution to firearms accidents is education. Firearms education programs can teach owners how to handle their guns properly; government regulation of the manufacturing of guns is not needed. Firearms companies insist that individuals need to take responsibility for their actions; if they leave loaded guns where children can find them, that's unfortunate but hardly the fault of the gun manufacturer.

According to the firearms industry, the cost of defending these lawsuits (or the addition of unwanted safety features) increases the price of guns and prevents poor people from being able to defend themselves. Gun manufacturers fear that these lawsuits will eventually bankrupt the industry or stop them from producing handguns at all. This would amount to a ban on the sale of handguns imposed not by the legislature, but by the courts.

Lawsuits over Distribution

More controversial than even the safety lawsuits are lawsuits attacking the ways that guns are distributed in the United States. These cases charge gun dealers with collective negligence by supplying a large black market which often puts guns in the hands of minors. The plaintiffs hope to use the courts to regulate firearms distribution in some way, such as by limiting gun sales to distributors who would sell only to major retail stores.

Governor Jeb Bush of Florida comments in defense of his signing into law (in 2001) a measure that would prevent local governments in his state from suing gun manufacturers. Most lawsuits against gun manufacturers are based on safety or distribution issues.

These lawsuits have received some credibility from the testimony of people within the firearms industry who chose to testify about distribution methods. For example, Robert Haas, a vice president of Smith & Wesson, stated in his affidavit in 1996 that gun manufacturers fully realize that

> the black market in firearms is not simply the result of stolen guns but is due to the seepage of guns into the illicit market from multiple thousands of unsupervised federal firearms licensees.... In spite of their knowledge, however, the industry's position has consistently been to take no independent action to insure responsible distribution practices.

A more dramatic example was the testimony of Robert Ricker, a former executive director of the American Shooting Sports Council (ASSC) and a former lawyer for the NRA. In 2003, he declared, "Instead of requiring dealers to be proactive and properly trained in an effort to stop questionable sales, it has been a common practice of gun manufacturers and distributors to adopt a 'see-no-evil, speak-no-evil' approach. This type of policy encourages a culture of evasion of firearms laws and regulations."

Gun manufacturers believe that these types of cases are illogical, the equivalent of holding a car manufacturer responsible for drunken driving deaths. A defense attorney stated that "there is no precedent in law that says Smith & Wesson is required to watch over its product for twenty years to make sure nothing happens to it." The solution, according to firearms companies, is stricter enforcement of criminal penalties for criminals.

Recent judicial decisions have supported the position of gun manufacturers. In *Young v. Bryco,* the father of nineteen-year-old Andrew Young is seeking legal action against Bryco Manufacturing and the gun dealers whose irresponsible distribution methods allowed two gang members to buy the semiautomatic Bryco 59 used to murder his son. Young was able to show a long-established

chain of sleazy distribution channels allowing guns to get to the gangs of Chicago. The judge, however, dismissed the case against the gun industry as a whole, ruling that the only true defendants were those specifically present in the chain of distribution of the murder weapon.

In July 1999, the National Association for the Advancement of Colored People (NAACP) filed a lawsuit (*NAACP v. Accu-Tek*) against several firearms manufacturers. The NAACP claimed that the distribution practices of firearms manufacturers caused handguns to end up in the hands of felons, leading to high levels of gun violence and resulting in a continuing public nuisance. The NAACP's case was unique, because it emphasized that this gun violence affected the African-American community far more than any other Americans. The NAACP did not seek monetary damages, but rather wanted increased gun safety programs and an injunction placing tougher restrictions on buyers and sellers of guns.

In May 2003, in Brooklyn, New York, an advisory jury for the case could not reach a verdict on twenty-three gun makers and dealers who have high ratios of gun sales to guns used in crime. The jury found the remaining forty-five

The president and CEO of the National Association for the Advancement of Colored People (NAACP), Kweisi Mfume (left), announced in 1999 that the organization would sue gun manufacturers, citing the damage done by guns to the African-American community in particular.

gun makers and distributors not liable in the case against the gun industry. The use of the courts to alter the practices of the firearms industry has generally not been effective.

Municipal Lawsuits

In November 1998, major cigarette manufacturers and the attorney generals of forty-six states signed a "master settlement agreement" in which the tobacco industry would pay the states $206 billion over twenty-five years. The agreement settled lawsuits by states against the tobacco industry but gave the industry no protection from liability in private lawsuits. The agreement did not depend on the action of Congress; the courts upheld it, and states began receiving money in November 1999.

A state representative in Oregon presents a bill before his legislature in 1999 that would prevent Oregon cities and counties from filing lawsuits against firearms manufacturers. Many such laws have been passed throughout the United States.

The success of these lawsuits led city and state governments to use a similar approach against the firearms industry. On October 30, 1998, New Orleans, Louisiana, became the first city to sue gun manufacturers for designing and marketing handguns that lack basic safety features such as safety locks, and for the failure to

develop and market smart guns. New Orleans mayor Marc Morial claimed that these safety features would prevent shootings by children, teenagers, and other unauthorized users. The city wanted gun manufacturers to pay for the city's share of the cost of police, emergency, and health care services due to gun injuries and deaths. Included in these costs were indirect damages, such as compensation for the treatment of gun-related injuries, police overtime, tax revenue lost through reduced worker productivity, and lower property values. At least thirty-three other cities and counties, including Cleveland, Ohio; Detroit, Michigan; and Miami, Florida, followed New Orleans's lead over the next year. Other city lawsuits, such as Chicago's, claim that the firearms industry is negligent in the way that it markets and distributes guns and that this negligence contributes to a massive illegal gun market.

Gun manufacturers lobbied state legislatures heavily to prevent these types of lawsuits from coming before judges and juries. For example, only eight months after New Orleans announced its lawsuit, the Louisiana state legislature passed Act 291. The act stated that no local government can bring "suit to recover...for damages for injury, death, or loss to seek other injunctive relief resulting from or relating to the lawful design, manufacture, marketing or sale of firearms." The legislature reserved this right to the state and then, amazingly, made the law retroactive (which means it would apply to any lawsuits that had begun before the law was passed). The city of New Orleans challenged the constitutionality of Act 291, and a lower district court ruled in favor of the city. The Louisiana Supreme Court, however, claimed by a five-to-two decision that the legislature had every right to make such a law and that New Orleans could not pursue the lawsuit. The U.S. Supreme Court refused to hear the case. Similar laws were passed in Georgia and Florida.

To date, most of the municipal cases that have reached the courts have not been successful anyway, although many are on appeal to higher courts. Judges in Cincinnati, Ohio; Bridgeport, Connecticut; and Miami dismissed suits. Dismissals in Chicago, New York State, and Gary, Indiana, are on appeal. Suits by Cleveland and by Newark and Jersey City in New Jersey have been allowed to proceed to pretrial fact-finding. Win or lose, the firearms industry claims that these suits have no merit, are expensive to defend, and threaten to bankrupt the industry.

Lorcin

A Kansas district attorney shows a .380 Lorcin handgun to a forensics specialist during a 2002 murder trial in the state. Inexpensive semiautomatic guns manufactured by Lorcin were the second most used guns in crimes, according to the Bureau of Alcohol, Tobacco and Firearms (BATF) in 1999.

In the early 1990s, Lorcin Engineering manufactured inexpensive (around $100), semiautomatic handguns known as Saturday night specials or junk guns. Lorcin was part of a group of six companies producing cheap guns in a "ring of fire" located within 45 miles (72 kilometers) of Los Angeles. Bryco (in Costa Mesa) and Davis Industries and Lorcin (both in Mira Loma) were three of the top five companies manufacturing handguns in America. In 1992, Lorcin made 180,000 cheap handguns; the six Los Angeles suburban firms together made 680,000 handguns.

Lorcin's semiautomatic pistol was used by many criminals; it finished second on the BATF's 1999 list of guns most frequently traced to crimes. In 1994, the company had also been involved in one of the largest gun theft cases in American history; Lorcin's own employees stole the company's guns, perhaps more than 10,000 of them, and then sold them to be used to commit crimes all around the United States. The president of Lorcin, James Waldorf, told a newspaper that "if someone wants to steal something bad enough, they're going to steal it....there has never been a gun that fired itself. The responsibility belongs with the individual." (Waldorf eventually went on to found another gun company in Nevada.)

In 1996, Lorcin told *Firearms Business* that it was declaring bankruptcy in order to "take advantage of the system" by avoiding the necessity of paying damages that might result from lawsuits. Other firearms manufacturers followed Lorcin's strategy. In 1999, Davis Industries also filed for bankruptcy protection. At a creditor's meeting, the owner was asked, "Now, the reasons for filing sounded to me like you're getting sued by all the municipalities in the United States. Is that pretty close to correct?" The representative for Davis responded, "I think you hit the button on the nose."

Democratic senator Carl Levin of Michigan proposed an amendment to bankruptcy legislation that would have prevented gun makers from declaring bankruptcy as a way to avoid the consequences of lawsuits filed against them by municipalities and individuals. In February 2000, by a vote of sixty-eight to twenty-nine, the Senate crushed this amendment. The NRA hailed the defeat of the Levin amendment as "a repudiation of the anti-gun agenda of junk lawsuits against gun makers."

Smith & Wesson Makes a Deal

In 2000, Smith & Wesson was the largest handgun manufacturer in the United States, producing more than 20 percent of the nation's handguns. In March, the company made a deal with the U.S. government, agreeing to a series of safety and business practice reforms. Smith & Wesson would limit its dealers to selling one gun per customer per day, install internal locking devices in all its guns within two years, and form a commission to make sure that the agreement was followed. In exchange, Smith & Wesson would be dismissed from some municipal lawsuits and avoid the possibility of crippling costs stemming from government lawsuits.

More controversially, Smith & Wesson also agreed that it would allow its weapons to be sold only by dealers who followed a strict "code of responsibility"—including background checks at gun shows—in all their gun sales (not just Smith & Wesson products). President Bill Clinton's administration hoped that other gun manufacturers would sign similar agreements, but in theory, the "code of responsibility" clause would influence the entire firearms industry, whether or not other manufacturers signed on. President Clinton called the agreement "a major victory for America's families."

In 2000, America's largest gun maker, Smith & Wesson, agreed to new safety measures that included child safety locks and smart gun technology in future designs.

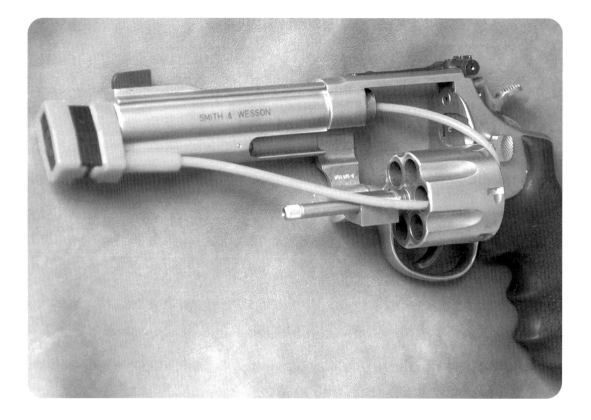

The Deal Unravels

Things began to go wrong with the agreement almost immediately. Some gun owners claimed that Smith & Wesson was sabotaging the entire industry. Many gun groups called for a boycott of Smith & Wesson products. One irate gun owner claimed that "the true intent of this agreement is to force down the throats of an entire lawful industry anti-gun policies rejected by the Congress, rejected by legislatures across America, and rejected by the judges." Smith & Wesson sales declined, perhaps as much as 40 percent.

Within two weeks, Smith & Wesson reinterpreted the agreement. The company now claimed that it had agreed to have its dealers make background checks only on buyers of Smith & Wesson products. "We can't agree to control things that we have no way to control," said a representative of Smith & Wesson. The U.S. government, however, stood by its interpretation that dealers who wanted to sell Smith & Wesson products had to impose the code's restrictions on buyers of all guns. A representative for the government claimed, "I think the language of the deal is clear on all these points."

To make matters worse for Smith & Wesson, other firearms companies refused to sign on. An attorney for Glock, one of the top handgun manufacturers in the United States, stated, "We will not subject ourselves to the monitoring of this commission." Nor would Browning bargain with the U.S. government over handgun safety. A representative from the firearms firm stated, "I would think that everybody in the country should be absolutely outraged, at not only Smith & Wesson's steps, but also the U.S. government's steps that have intruded into the legislative process."

At the time, Smith & Wesson was owned by Tomkins, a massive British corporation. Tomkins, under some pressure in Britain for owning the firearms company in the first place, clearly misunderstood the cultural significance of guns in America. The company thought that it was making a simple deal to install safety locks and follow other government instructions in return for being dismissed from municipal lawsuits against the gun industry. Surprised by the aggravation of owning a firearms company in America, Tomkins promptly sold Smith & Wesson to Saf-T-Hammer, an Arizona-based firm, for $15 million. Tomkins had paid $113 million for the company. The Clinton administration threatened to sue Smith & Wesson to force the gun company to comply with the agreement, but no lawsuit was ever filed. The deal between the U.S. government and Smith & Wesson turned out to be a dead end.

Legal Immunity for the Gun Industry?

Although firearms manufacturers claimed that the lawsuits against the industry had no legal merit, they feared that juries, listening to grieving relatives of gunshot victims, would rule against the industry, regardless of the law. At first, the manufacturers lobbied state legislatures to pass laws that created legal immunity from liability exclusively for the gun industry. A national bill that would

Two U.S. representatives hold a press conference in 1999 on behalf of the Law Enforcement Alliance opposing President Bill Clinton's gun control legislation. They are accompanied by cardboard cutouts of police officers, which represent police support of their position.

limit lawsuits against the industry by local governments and private citizens stood little chance to survive a sure veto from President Clinton. As governor of Texas, however, George W. Bush had signed a similar law. With the presidency and—after 2002—both houses of Congress in the control of the Republican Party (which is generally more sympathetic to the firearms industry than the Democratic Party), the time seemed right to push this strategy on a national level.

On April 9, 2003, the U.S. House of Representatives passed HR 1036, the so-called Protection of Legal Commerce in Arms Act, by a 285–140 vote (221–3 among Republicans). It states that no one can bring a lawsuit in any state or federal court against a manufacturer or seller of firearms or ammunition for damages or injunctive relief resulting from the unlawful acts of people who misuse guns. The bill specifies certain types of lawsuits that would still be allowable, including those against a person who transfers a gun, knowing that it will be used to commit a violent crime, and actions for damages resulting directly from a defect in design or manufacture of a firearm, when used as intended. This bill covers only licensed manufacturers and sellers.

S 659, a similar bill sponsored by Republican senator Larry Craig of Idaho, will be debated in the U.S. Senate, where Democrats implied that they would do everything in their power to prevent its passage. Democratic senator Richard Durbin of Illinois claimed that the legislation was an example of "sordid...special interest sleaze."

The Bush administration claimed that legal immunity "would help prevent abuse of the legal system and help curb the growing problem of frivolous lawsuits in the United States" that were damaging honest, legitimate weapons suppliers. Advocates of immunity legislation claim that such lawsuits are a plot to bankrupt the gun industry and achieve gun control or even handgun prohibition. The federal and state governments, not the courts, have the power to regulate the gun industry if they choose. According to HR 1036 supporters, the gun industry requires protection in order to prevent people from blaming manufacturers and dealers when a criminal misuses a gun.

The Case Against Legal Immunity

Opponents of HR 1036 claim that this type of law would completely rewrite legal principles that have existed for centuries. They argue that the lawsuits against the firearms industry have nothing to do with regulation or banning guns, but simply attempt to compensate innocent victims and encourage responsible conduct. Holding gun companies liable for increasing the risk of injury from misuse makes all parties who contributed to the harm responsible for their own conduct; it does not shift the blame away from other guilty parties. Similarly, laws punish the automobile manufacturer who could have made the car safer but do not prevent actions against drunken drivers. One former NRA attorney alleged that lawsuits provide a crucial tool for motivating the industry to reform and act responsibly. Opponents of legal immunity for the gun industry question why the industry is the only business that requires special protection. If Congress is concerned about the role of courts in American society, it should limit negligence suits against all businesses. The fact that it doesn't indicates the power of the special interest gun lobby.

No End to the Debate in Sight

In 2003, Democratic senator Barbara Mikulski of Maryland stated that if the firearms immunity bill passes, the families of the victims of the sniper attacks in the Washington, D.C., area in 2002 would be barred by Congress from suing the Tacoma, Washington, gun shop that sold the gun to the alleged snipers. The shop has no record of that sale or the sales of more than 200 other guns. The victims' families believe the shop was negligent.

Senator Barbara Mikulski of Maryland, shown here in May 2003, pointed out that the firearms immunity bill would prevent families of the victims of the 2002 sniper attacks in the Washington, D.C., area from suing the shop in Washington state that sold the gun used in the crimes.

However, Chris Cox, chief lobbyist for the NRA, says that the bill only protects legal manufacturers from being held responsible for the illegal actions of criminals. Cox asserted, "It doesn't protect those who break state or federal laws. It doesn't close the door to anyone" filing claims against wrongdoers.

Like almost all legislation regarding guns, the firearms immunity bill is extremely controversial. Regardless of whether or not it passes, the debate over the responsibility of the firearms industry for deaths caused by guns is not likely to end anytime soon.

Glossary

advocacy group—an organization that seeks to persuade people to support a particular viewpoint on a public issue, such as for or against increased restrictions on gun use

amendment—a change or addition to a legal document, such as an amendment to the U.S. Constitution

armory—a place where arms are manufactured

arsenal—a place for storing war supplies, including weapons

assassination—the premeditated killing of a person, usually a public figure

assault weapons—antipersonnel rifles, shotguns, and handguns designed mainly for military and law enforcement purposes

automatic weapon—a weapon that fires more than one round with a single pull of the trigger

caliber—a measurement of the inside of a gun barrel

cartridge—a case that holds the primer and bullet; also, the case, primer, and bullet all together

crime rate—the amount of crime, presented in statistical terms

division of labor—a manufacturing process in which the production of something is divided into a series of specialized steps, each completed by a large number of people

firearm—a weapon that uses a powder charge to shoot something, usually a bullet or shell, from a straight tube

gun control—restrictions on the use and ownership of guns

homicide—murder

legal immunity—protection from legal responsibility

liability—legal obligation or responsibility

magazine—the container in a firearm that stores the cartridges before they pass into the chamber for firing; also a storehouse for gunpowder and ammunition

militia—a military organization made up of people who are not professional soldiers

munitions—weapons and ammunition

ordnance—weapons, ammunition, and other military equipment

poll—a sampling of public opinion

round—a single shot from a firearm; a cartridge

self-defense—an action by an individual to protect himself or herself

semiautomatic weapon—a weapon that reloads automatically after firing, although the trigger must be pulled to fire each round

Bibliography

Books

Anderson, Jervis. *Guns in American Life*. New York: Random House, 1984.

Dizard, Jan, et al. *Guns in America: A Reader*. New York: New York University Press, 1999.

Ellis, John. *The Social History of the Machine Gun*. New York: Pantheon, 1975.

Garavaglia, Louis, and Charles Worman. *Firearms of the American West, 1803–1865*. Albuquerque: University of New Mexico Press, 1984.

Hagerman, Edward. *The American Civil War and the Origins of Modern Warfare*. Bloomington: Indiana University Press, 1988.

Hosley, William. *Colt: The Making of an American Legend*. Amherst: University of Massachusetts Press, 1996.

Slotkin, Richard. *Gunfighter Nation: The Myth of the Frontier in Twentieth-Century America*. New York: Atheneum, 1985.

Utter, Glenn. *Encyclopedia of Gun Control and Gun Rights*. Westport, CT: Greenwood Press, 1999.

Web Sites

ArmsCollectors.com—Important Dates in Gun History *www.armscollectors.com/gunhistorydates.htm*

Colt *www.colt.com*

Harpers Ferry National Historical Park *www.nps.gov/hafe/home.htm*

The Institute for Research on Small Arms in International Security (IRSAIS) *www.smallarmsresearch.org*

Remington *www.remington.com*

Smith & Wesson *www.smith-wesson.com*

Springfield Armory National Historic Site *www.nps.gov/spar/home.html*

Index

Note: Page numbers in *italics* indicate illustrations and captions.